# This Is the
# DREAMING

## Australian Aboriginal Legends

*Jean Ellis, who grew up in central western New South Wales (Wiradjuri territory), has had a long and close association with Aboriginal people from many different areas and from all walks of life. She has shared their idividual triumphs and their many setbacks. Most significantly, sha has shared their quest for recognition, understanding, and reconciliation.*

*Over many years of contact, Jean has encouraged Aboriginal people to speak freely of their heritage and culture, and to treasure their traditional languages and their Dreaming legends.*

*Some of the legends presented in this book are well known throughout Australia; others have come from Jean's personal, authenticated collection. Together they display a fascinating mixture of human emotions and reactions: love, desire, jealousy, caution, kindness, friendship, bitterness, and understanding.*

*Jean Ellis is also the author of* From the Dreamtime *and* Australia's Aboriginal Heritage, *published by Collins Dove.*

*Clive 'Bidja' Atkinson was born at Mooroopna, Victoria, and is a descendant of the Yorta Yorta tribe that has inhabited the Murray/Goulburn River region for over 40,000 years. Clive's style is contemporary yet based on his ancestral homeland, and uses strong imagery and earth colors. Through his art Clive aims to promote understanding and appreciation of Australia's Aboriginal culture.*

# This Is the
# DREAMING

## Australian Aboriginal Legends

## Jean A Ellis

CollinsDove
An imprint of HarperCollins*Publishers*

Published by Collins Dove
An imprint of HarperCollins*Religious*
A member of the HarperCollins*Publishers* (Australia) Pty Ltd group
(ACN 008 431 730)
22–24 Joseph Street
North Blackburn, Victoria 3130, Australia

First published 1994
Reprinted 1995
Designed by William Hung
Cover design by William Hung
Cover illustration by Clive Atkinson
Illustrations by Clive Atkinson

Typeset by Collins Dove
Printed in Australia by Griffin Paperbacks

The National Library of Australia
Cataloguing-in-Publication Data:

Ellis, Jean A.
This is the dreaming: Australian Aboriginal legends.

Includes index
ISBN 86371 291 7

[1.] Aborigines, Australian – Legends. [2.] Aborigines,
Australian – Folklore. I. Title.

398.2049915

# Contents

**To the Aboriginal People of Australia
to whom these legends belong**

Many people have collaborated in the making
of this book and the author and publisher wish
to express their thanks to:

the Aboriginal people whose legends are
here retold;

the artist Clive Atkinson, whose drawings
do so much to enhance the stories;

Anne Boyd, who edited the legends;

Erin Fowler, whose encouragement, advice
and typing were much appreciated.

# Preface

Australia is an ancient land—an isolated land of mystery and great extremes. The Aboriginal people, whose presence in Australia goes back beyond human reckoning, have become part of its soul, its mystique, its spiritual force.

These people, who once numbered more than five hundred thousand, lived for tens of thousands of years in this land. They were isolated from other land masses, other civilisations and in most instances, from each other. This did not concern them.

To each individual, to each group, the land itself was the nurturer, their mother, the giver of all things needed. These people looked not for change. Their lives had purpose, substance and joy. We can glimpse this through a study of their vivid, vibrant oral history.

From all areas across Australia there has come an ever-growing, incredibly complex collection of exciting legends. Some are spirit-given and sacred beyond contemporary understanding. Some are records of incidents and times long passed. Some were presented originally as parables; as part of the cultural and spiritual learning program of the Traditional period. Others were created by skilled storytellers and chanted or dramatised as part of an entertaining corroboree presentation.

Today, we are unable to know or fully understand the initial purpose or spiritual link of each legend, but through them we can certainly share the strong and varied emotions, the excitement, the fear, the joy of the people. Through the legends we can certainly feel and recognise Australia's very strong Aboriginal heritage.

The legends presented in this book represent only a small fraction of the whole. They were selected from several, separate tribal areas and written to suit publication needs. A sincere endeavour has been made to retain and portray the raw Aboriginality, the true essence of each.

Jean A Ellis

# DREAMING

All the triumph
The tragedy
Of each yesteryear
Seems somehow to stay, forever quite near.
This is the Dreaming.

Tomorrow
Will dawn.
A tomorrow that's clear,
A tomorrow that is not shadowed by fear.
This is the Dreaming.

# Rainbow-colored Birds

*This enchanting story has come from the Bardi
people who live in the area where Broome,
Western Australia stands today. As with most
legends it carries a message. The story, though it
has come from the distant past, is still told by story
tellers today and is a favorite with all children,
Aboriginal and non Aboriginal alike. It tells how
the birds of Australia became so wonderfully
multi-colored.*

In the very early days of the Dreaming, when the birds and animals were first created, all the birds, every different species, every different size, had feathers that were black—plain, dull, black! The birds looked very ordinary and bleak indeed as they busily flitted about. There came a time, however, when this was changed forever.

The change began on a bright, sunshiny morning when a small black dove was flying around in search of food. The little dove very soon spotted a juicy worm so he dived from the sky to snatch it from its hole. As he landed, his tiny foot was pricked by a sharp splinter from a nearby log. Immediately the wound began to bleed and the bird fell down and rolled onto his back. He lay there crying piteously for help.

Within minutes, birds of many kinds came swooping in from all over the area and gathered protectively around him, anxious to help. Some carried water in their beaks to drop into the little dove's mouth. Others

washed the wound and tried to stop the bleeding with a poultice of leaves. Some of the larger birds perched on a high branch so that their bodies cast a blanket of shade over the little dove. Each one fussed and worried and wondered what else they could do to help. All of them, that is, except for the crow.

The big, black crow strutted around impatiently, telling the others in no uncertain terms to go mind their own business. It didn't concern the crow that the injured little bird might very likely die—and soon. The crow, it seems, was always cross, but on this occasion he was especially so. He was angry because the fluttering of wings, the flying to and fro and the anxious chatter of the birds had disturbed his peace and quiet. He didn't like it, one bit.

Eventually the mean thing decided to get really savage. He fluffed out his feathers, flapped his wings and shrieked angrily as he flew hard, right at the others, hoping to frighten them all away. The friendly birds were disturbed by this, but though they scattered, they still hovered close by. Each one tried to ignore the crow as they wondered what more they could do to help the stricken little dove.

Sadly, however, despite their concern, the wound was becoming more inflamed by the minute. Very soon they noticed that the foot of the little dove had swollen to three times its normal size. What could be done?

Suddenly a galah, who was known for her quick thinking, and also for her sharp beak, flew down to the dying little bird. The others watched in horror as she

pecked at the injured foot and the unhappy little bird cried out in terrible pain. Then suddenly, magically, the pain disappeared and the gathering of birds watched in amazement as a beautiful, wondrous thing, such as they had never seen before, began to happen.

They had expected that lots of pus, dried blood and other gucky stuff would ooze from the wound, but no; instead, a great stream of magical, marvelous, magnificent colors spilled out. The many colors, which were in liquid form, dripped and splashed onto the amazed birds. Splashes of the pink, light grey and pure white fell onto the galah. She shrieked with delight, as she danced about, admiring herself. Great spurts of yellow, purple, blue, green and red with more and more white splashed onto each of the others. There was great excitement.

Some birds found themselves drenched all over with one particular color; others were covered with yet another; while others still, were surprised to discover that they had been splashed by many different colors. The lorikeets for instance, looked like a whole rainbow in themselves! What an exciting, wonderful experience it was for all of them. On top of all this, the little dove began to feel much improved. This was the best thing of all.

The happy little bird, who found he had suddenly become white, a lovely pure white all over, began to dance around in delight.

It was a very special day for all the birds. Somehow each one knew that it would be able to keep new and beautiful colors for ever.

As you have no doubt realised, the birds had been given their new colors as a reward for all the kindness they had shown to the dove, and magically at this time, the colors of every other bird throughout this wide, brown land, changed, too. All, that is, except for the crow. The terrible, bad-tempered old crow was not touched in any way by this special magic. The crow was black as he had always been.

He and all of his kind have remained that way ever since.

# The Gaya-Dari Twins
## or
# How the Platypus Came to Be

*This legend comes from the Euahlayi people whose area covered much of the north-western area of New South Wales. Some people think of it as a jokey sort of story but there is sadness in it too, sadness for a little mother who had children who didn't belong.*

In the very early days of Australia, as the first people were beginning to move away from the coast and the first animals were finding their true habitats, there lived a group of ducks. They were each very timid and shied away from contact with all other creatures. The ducks lived in a select place on the banks of a large river. They were content and peaceful and very few ever ventured away.

Eventually, though, one of the very young ducks grew a little tired of this. She would often gaze into the distance wondering how far the waters of the great river flowed. Each day she ventured a little further along the river looking around at the oh so beautiful world. Of course when she returned each night the others in her group scolded her.

'It is not safe,' they warned. 'You must stay close to us or something bad might happen.' The little duck always laughed at them.

'It's a wonderful world,' she would answer. 'Nothing

bad could ever happen. Please stop fussing.' When morning came she would happily go adventuring yet again.

If the truth be known she was being a little foolish, for an evil water spirit called Mulloka hovered around that area. He was known, in times past, to have captured young ducks and those he had captured had never been seen again! The older ducks worried about the little duck constantly but she, as young creatures have always done, refused to believe that there was any danger.

One very bright, sparkling day she decided to swim far, far down the river, further than ever before. When the sun was high in the sky she decided to rest in the warm sunshine on the seemingly peaceful bank. She settled into a comfortable spot on the soft grass, feeling very happy and very proud of herself.

Suddenly the peaceful, relaxed atmosphere was shattered as a thick net of vines fell down upon her. She jumped to her feet and began squawking and quacking loudly as she frantically struggled to free herself.

'Stop your noise, you stupid little duck,' said a loud booming voice. 'I am the great Mulloka. You are now my prisoner. You will never ever escape from me. It is useless to struggle. So—be quiet and be still.' When the little duck heard these words she felt herself grow numb with fear. She trembled and sobbed because she could see no way out of the terrible situation.

Then like a miracle she saw that help had arrived. She saw that a friendly creature had come to save her.

It was a giant water rat. He was old and ugly but the little duck didn't mind. She was very pleased to see him, whatever he looked like.

The fierce old rat bit the leg of Mulloka, using his sharp teeth, then he dug his little spears—those which were attached to his hind legs—into Mulloka's bare feet. With an angry cry of pain the evil spirit-man let go of the net, dropping the little duck so that he could dive at the rat!

Quick as a flash, the little duck seized this opportunity and scrambled free. She then flapped her wings and ran and waddled, as fast as she could, though she didn't know where. Soon she realized that the rat, who had easily avoided Mulloka's clumsy clutches, was running along beside her. They could both hear big, old Mulloka as he chased wildly after them, bellowing all the while.

The two hurried along breathlessly for several minutes. Then the water rat screamed, 'Quick. Follow me.' As he shouted he clambered down into a deep, dark opening in the earth. Without thought or hesitation the little duck clambered after him. Down, down into the blackness she went. She was very glad when finally she found soft earth below. It was really good to rest and catch her breath, though the place she was in seemed to be very dark and musty.

When she felt better she looked around the dimly lit tunnel. It was cold and somewhat scary. She was thinking how dark and dismal it was when the rat said proudly, 'This is my home.'

The little duck was surprised and shocked but

somehow she managed to make her voice sound friendly, as she thanked the old rat for rescuing her. Then she added, 'You were kind and clever, but now I must go home.' Having said this, she began to waddle toward the entrance but, in an instant, the water rat sprang up and barred her way.

'No,' he said firmly. 'You will not be going home. I am tired of living alone. I am going to keep you here with me forever.'

'Oh no. No! No! No!' shrieked the little duck. 'I don't want to stay with you. I must go. I must go!'

At this point the old rat became angry. His beady, black eyes began to blaze fiercely and he bared his sharp, pointy teeth. He then reached out with his front foot and cuffed the little duck across the head.

'I saved you from Mulloka,' he hissed. 'I saved you and now you are *my* prisoner.' The little duck felt desperately upset. She flopped down on the cold, moist earth and sobbed.

'If you are sensible and quiet I will not hurt you,' said the rat more gently, 'But if you fight me or make that dreadful quacking noise ever again I will bite and beat you badly.' He then bared his sharp teeth one more time as he looked menacingly down at her. The little duck could see that it was useless to argue further. She felt defeated and very sad.

As the days passed she tried hard not to annoy the mean old rat because she was quite afraid of him. All the while however she dreamed of her escape. Most of the time, he kept her locked up in his deep, dark, tunnel home but just occasionally he let her out for a

quick swim. During these times, he watched her very closely and reminded her of the horrid things he would do if she dared to try to escape.

It was a terrible life but somehow the little duck survived. She was determined to live through it all in the hope that one day, one marvelous day, she would find a way to be free once again. And she did.

Because the little duck appeared always to be co-operative and quiet the crabby old rat began to believe that she must now like living in his home, and gradually he became a little less strict. One day when he had let her out for a swim, he actually relaxed, closed his eyes, and lay back on the river bank in the warm sun. The little duck, as always, was watching.

As soon as she saw the old rat nodding off to sleep she quickly but very quietly swam to the bank. Once there, she scrambled out, shook her feathers, and then began to waddle as fast as she could through the thick bushland towards her home.

When the rat finally opened his eyes he was surprised and angry to find that she was gone. At first he thought she might have been caught in underwater vines, so he dived to the bottom of the river and searched for her. He searched and searched but she could not be found. He then swam quickly to the surface and looked into the distance in both directions. No little duck could be seen.

'Darn,' he said. 'Evil old Mulloka must have got her after all. Darn! Darn! Darn!' The old rat scurried back into his empty hole muttering angrily to himself.

Meanwhile the little duck was flip-flapping her

clumsy wings and scrambling through and over bushes in her panicky, desperate effort to get home. She didn't seem to feel the pain as brambles and such reached out and scratched her. When she eventually arrived home the other ducks were amazed but very happy to see her. They quickly gathered around. They gave her water and food and put soothing oils on her scratched and bleeding body.

Days passed and the little duck gradually became well and strong. She was very happy indeed to be safely back and she knew she would never ever want to go adventuring again.

Very soon after her arrival home several of the other young ducks began to make nests for themselves. The little duck decided to make a nest too. She was extremely proud and pleased when, just like the others, she found she was able to lay two beautiful duck eggs in her warm little nest. She cared for the eggs well and sat on them lovingly as a good little mother duck should.

In the prescribed time the various batches of eggs began to hatch and one by one the other ducks proudly paraded their new, fluffy, little ducklings for all to see. Eventually the little duck's babies also hatched but, oh dear, she did not want to show her babies off. She did not want the other ducks to see them because they were not soft, fluffy and pretty. Her babies were strange-looking, little creatures, very, very strange indeed!

They were gaya-dari creatures. Instead of soft, yellow feathers, they had bristly, brown fur. Though their feet

were webbed as they should be, and their bills were those of a duck, instead of having two feet, they had four! It was terrible. And what is more, each of their hind legs was already showing the tip of a sharp little spear, just like the spears on the water rat's hind legs.

The little duck loved her babies dearly but she was afraid to let the other ducks see them. Eventually, though, she was forced to lead them out of the nest because they needed to practise their swimming skills.

As the little duck feared, when she appeared with her two strange babies, there was a commotion such as had never been heard before. The other ducks were horrified.

'Get those creatures away from here,' they hissed. 'Get them away! Get them away! We will kill them. We will kill them if they stay! Get them away! They are monsters!'

The little duck was very upset. Her babies did not understand what was happening. They were confused and frightened. They hid behind their mother. The little duck was confused and frightened herself, but very quickly she realised what she must do. She knew she must take her gaya-dari babies far, far away and raise them, somehow, on her own. She thought of asking the water rat for help but then decided against it. She knew that he, like the ducks, would be angry if he saw such odd little creatures at his door.

The little duck and her babies, bravely but most unhappily, set out. They traveled up the river for many

days. At the base of the mountain they found a warm cave and there they decided to stay.

Weeks and months slowly passed and the babies grew up strong and well. Though she was pleased to see this, the little mother was almost always sad and melancholy. She missed her duck people very much even though they had, in the end, turned against her. She was disappointed too, because, as her babies grew up they became even less like her. Worst of all was the fact that her two babies had dug, and then lived in, a deep dark tunnel home, just like the water rat. Her children had begged her to share the tunnel with them but she could not. After all, she was a duck and she needed to see the sky and the trees and breathe the fresh air. Eventually, because she had so many problems, the sad little duck pined away and died.

Her children were sad but they lived on. At times, they were lonely and frightened, but eventually these two had babies, which hatched out and looked exactly like their parents. This made the parents feel better.

As the years passed, more such little babies were hatched and grew, so that with time, there were a great many gaya-dari creatures. The gaya-daris, as their numbers increased, ventured forth into many different areas, right across the land. They made their homes by burrowing into the banks of rivers and other waterways. Eventually they became a common sight.

Gaya-dari of course, in the language of the Euahlayi people, means platypus!

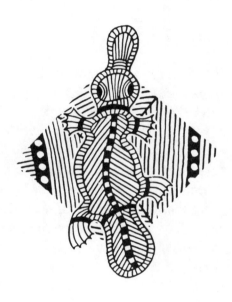

# The Owl Who was Unwelcome

*Way back in the days of the Dreaming several different Aboriginal groups lived on separate sections of the Western Australian coast. This legend comes from the Worona people who lived on the banks of a river, now known as Fitzroy River, near to where Derby is today. It tells how these people were able to live very comfortably, with nature providing their every need. In actual fact, it seems that the lives of the Worona people became a little too comfortable and some of them became uncaring, cruel and thoughtless.*

The children of the Worona were well cared for and very happy. Each day they would play along the river bank, laughing and squealing with glee. One day, one of the boys went for a walk in a nearby forest. As he returned he excitedly called out, 'Come quickly everyone. I have found a strange, new bird. It has large peering eyes, and a loud unusual call.'

'Come quickly,' he called a second time. 'Come and see this bird before it flies away.' All of the children, and most of the adults too, hurriedly followed the boy as he led them to the strange, new bird.

It was an owl. It was the very first owl that had ever lived on earth. The great Wandjina, the god of that area, had sent one of his spirits in the form of the owl.

As an owl, the spirit was to observe the people in this area and report back to Wandjina, letting him know if there was anything more that could be done for these fortunate and favored people. The people, of course, were unaware of this.

When the owl first saw the great crowd emerge from the bush he was surprised but pleased. He watched in amusement as several boys began to climb his tree, reaching out towards him as they came closer. The owl had no fear of the boys or any of these people. He expected that he would be patted and petted and taken back to their camp site where he would be cared for and treasured as a novelty. How wrong he was!

You can imagine his horror and shock when suddenly he was whacked severely and knocked from his perch. As soon as he hit the ground the owl knew that his wing was badly damaged and he would therefore be unable to escape. The people all stared at the helpless, quivering bird as he lay there on the ground. No one protested or tried to assist him. Some of the children then decided to toss him into the air. Each one took a turn. Over and over again they tossed him up, and they all laughed as they watched him fall, again and again.

They were treating the owl like a toy, as if he had no feelings. They seemed to think that, because he was new and so totally different to any bird they had seen before, he somehow wasn't real. We know, of course, that the owl was very real indeed and the poor creature was soon in terrible pain as his frail little bones became battered and broken.

You would think that the cruel children would stop at this point, but they did not. When they were tired of tossing him into the air they began to pull out his feathers. And believe it or not, the adults thought that

this was funny. The unfortunate owl could not get away. He was totally at their mercy and they, it seems, had none to give.

The owl felt very disappointed as he suffered in silence. He knew that he had come to these people from the great Wandjina with the thought of giving care, extra help and guidance. In return he had received only cruelty and mockery. This distressed him even more than the pain of his wounds. It was a very disturbing situation and what's more worse was yet to come.

'We can't have a bird without feathers,' called a half-grown boy mockingly. 'So let's give him some new ones,' he said as he stuck a sharply pointed blade of spinifex grass into the twitching, bleeding little body of the owl. The other children needed little encouragement.

'What fun,' they all decided and soon the distressed owl was covered with spinifex blades, each one driven hard in, so that they stuck out grotesquely from his dying little body. The boy who had thought of the spinifex idea, then tossed the owl into the air, one final time.

'Go on, strange creature,' he shouted. 'We have given you new feathers, so let's see you fly.' Everyone laughed as they watched the lifeless little body soar upwards. They expected that the battered owl would soon fall with a thud to the ground. The people all watched and waited. They watched, laughing as they waited.

Suddenly their laughter ceased. Their laughter ceased and the eyes of every person opened wide in amazement for the battered, blood-streaked bird

somehow managed to flap his broken wings. He did not fall to the ground but managed, tentatively, to stay aloft. Then, as they continued to watch, the bird began to fly, strong and free, away beyond the clouds and out of sight. Wandjina had caused this to happen.

The great Wandjina had looked down and had seen what was happening. He had instantly taken all pain from the owl and beckoned him up to the sky world.

The people below stood about for a time, looking up in bewilderment. As they watched and wondered, they heard a loud, low moan of sadness from the sky. This was followed by a mighty, very angry roar, such as they had never heard before. It was, of course, the great Wandjina, showing his concern and extreme disappointment. The people began to realize that they had done wrong and they grew frightened.

And well they might, for Wandjina was very angry indeed! He could not believe that his special people would be so uncaring. How dare they be so cruel simply because the owl was new and different! Though it saddened him, he decided that these people must be punished, most severely.

Wandjina quickly summoned a fierce wind to blow and vivid flashes of lightning to light up the sky. He pushed and punched the murky, misty clouds as he sought to create a wild and terrible storm. The storm soon began and the rain fell on these people more heavily than it had ever fallen before. It fell ceaselessly all that day and for days and days to come. Very soon the water in the river rose and began flooding out across the plain. Still the rain continued to fall, and

the flood water rose higher and higher, surging towards the sea.

The people tried desperately to find high places where they would be safe but the flood water continued to rise till it reached each one of them. Eventually almost every man, woman and child in that group was sucked into the swirling torrent of water and drowned.

Only one man and one woman survived. These two had managed to grab the tail of a kangaroo as it had struggled through the flood to safety. They had hung on desperately and eventually the kangaroo had dragged them inland to dry ground. Once they realized they were safe the man and woman had much to be grateful for and much to think about. They had learned their lesson well. They knew that they must never again be so cruel and foolish. They knew too that they must never again make Wandjina angry. And they didn't!

These two became the first of a new and much more caring group of Worona people.

Many centuries have passed since then and many thousands more Worona people have lived, generation after generation, in this place. Each new generation of people has been told this story and never again has anyone ever harmed an owl, many of which now live very safely there. In addition, the new Worona people have developed a deep understanding of, and respect for, all living creatures and all other peoples too, regardless of differences.

Wandjina is now very well pleased indeed.

# The Sisters Who Lived in the Sea

*This legend comes from the Wirango people who lived, in the Traditional period, on the coast of South Australia. As you would expect, it is a story about the ocean and tells how the first shark came to be and why the evening star shines so brightly.*

We are told that during the mystical Dreaming era, two sisters in the Wirango area lived like mermaids in the depths of the ocean. Remember that, during this period, the people could, if they wished, adopt the form and mannerisms of their individual totem animal.

It is said that the girls sheltered in caves which had been formed by the great underwater kelp mounds. Though they were quite content to live under the water, they enjoyed an occasional trip to the surface where they would resume their human form.

Each sister was very beautiful and very graceful. Whenever they were on the beach they made a very pretty picture as they ran along the soft sand, laughing together and singing. The girls enjoyed searching among the rocks and on the sand for crabs and pipis. They considered these to be a special delicacy and they often lit a fire and cooked them before returning to their ocean home.

On one such occasion, as they were relaxing in the

warm sunshine, the two were noticed by a lone hunter. His name was Koolulla. Though he was a clever hunter and fisherman he was not well liked by his own people because he was often mean and cruel. He was also a fiercely determined man who seemed to constantly argue with everyone around him.

On this particular day he was carrying his spear, his firestick and a large fishing net and he was careful to stand quietly, keeping well out of sight as he spied on the two girls. He had never before seen two such beautiful girls. He was fascinated and very soon decided that he would capture both of them and keep them as his wives.

As you can imagine, the girls were surprised and shocked when suddenly they looked up and saw Koolulla running wildly towards them. Before either one could manage to escape, he dropped his huge fishing net over them both and began to secure it. Both girls struggled violently. Eventually the younger one broke free and immediately ran, as fast as she could, back towards the sea.

Koolulla was, of course, very angry! As quickly as possible, he knotted the net tightly around the older girl; then he chased after the younger one. As he ran he dropped his firestick which sprayed red sparks and flames into the afternoon sky, creating a vivid red glow. Because Koolulla was strong and could run quite fast he very nearly caught up with the younger girl, but once she reached the ocean, he had no hope. This girl could swim like a fish! And what's more, once she was in the water, her lungs, as always, were

instantly and magically changed. She was able to dive, down, down, down, like a real sea creature, to the safety of the forests of kelp. There she hid, quivering with fear.

Koolulla, who had followed her into the water, did not know that she had special powers and so he swam about searching frantically for her. He could not understand how she could possibly have disappeared in such a short time and he worked himself into a terrible rage. He could not believe that such a slim young girl could possibly out-run and also out-swim him!

As time passed his rage became so uncontrollable that he lost all reason. He began thrashing wildly about in the water, diving more deeply than he should, while his brain began to fill with terrible thoughts of violence and vengeance. He stubbornly refused to give up the search and swim back to shore and safety. Eventually he felt that he must be drowning; his chest began to ache as if it would burst and his legs and arms became paralyzed. Suddenly, however, the pain ceased and a strange feeling began to spread through him, as his body began to change shape completely.

Within minutes Koolulla found that he was no longer a human man. The ancestor spirits, who were angry with his behavior, had caused him to become a very large sea creature; the kind we know today as a shark. He had become the very first shark.

While all this was happening, the girl was huddling, frightened, alone and in tears, in her underwater cave. She was, of course, very concerned about her sister. She reasoned, though, that Koolulla would have taken

her sister away by now, so she considered that a rescue attempt would be useless.

We know of course, that the unfortunate, older girl had not been taken away. She was still on the beach and sadly, she was still trapped in the fishing net! This story might have had a different ending if only the younger girl had decided to go up to the beach and investigate. But she did not, and so the elder girl was left there struggling desperately. All day she struggled and cried out for help, but no one heard her; no one came.

Eventually, when she was totally exhausted, a numb feeling came upon her and she was still. She lay that way for another day before her heart finally ceased to beat. As she died an ancestor spirit carried her gently to the sky-world.

'You were brave and kind while you lived,' he told her 'so I have decided, that, from now, your goodness will shine, shine as an example for all the world to see.'

The girl did not at first understand what he meant but in the twinkling of an eye she found she had been magically transformed into a brightly shining, beautiful star. She became the star we now call the 'evening star'. When the people on earth looked up and saw the newest star they were pleased.

Many weeks later, the younger girl, who was still very frightened and upset, summoned up enough courage to go up, once again, to the surface. She took her coolamon with her. Quickly she gathered fresh pipis, made a fire and roasted them. As she nibbled at

the pipis she watched the daylight fading. When she saw the red glow of sunset, tears filled her eyes. She was reminded of cruel Koolulla and the firestick he had dropped. The girl was overcome with sadness for she still grieved deeply for her lost sister.

Suddenly, through her tears, she saw a new, brightly shining star appear. As she watched, the star seemed to glow especially brightly, just for her, and a warm, peaceful feeling came upon her. In that instant she knew that the star was the spirit of her sister who had somehow been magically and wonderfully transformed. As she gazed up at the star she felt far less lonely. It was very comforting to realize that her sister would be there, for all time, to watch over her.

And that is how it continued to be.

Since that time, so very long ago, many other girls, in need of guidance and reassurance, have found the comfort they needed, while sitting quietly, looking up at this brightly shining, beautiful evening star.

Next time you see pipis on the beach, or look up at the evening star, you may perhaps think of this story. I always do.

# The Friends Who Couldn't be Parted

*This legend comes from the Wutati people on the north coast of Queensland where the didgeridoo was, and still is, played prolifically during feasts and corroborees. The land of the Wutati people is also an area where possums and crabs are found in large numbers.*

THE FRIENDS WHO COULDN'T BE PARTED

In the language of the Wutati, of coastal far north Queensland, the word 'rurera' means crab and the word 'parray' means possum. A long, long time ago, however, when the world was still in the Dreaming stage, these were the names of two young Wutati men who lived in this area.

The two had grown up together. They had been close friends from the time they were both very young. One seldom went anywhere or did anything without the other. During the day they would hunt together, help to make canoes and implements together, or fish and swim in the ocean together. During the night they would mostly be found entertaining the people of their group. This they did together too.

Both men had a definite talent for entertaining. Rurera was a dancer. He could leap and step and dance incredibly well. His people loved to watch him. He danced always to the dreeing of the didgeridoo which was played by his friend Parray.

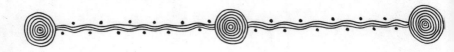

Parray was accepted as the very best didgeridoo player that there ever had been. He had many different didgeridoos and could create all manner of sounds and rhythms while playing them. Over the years his fame had spread and the people of many other groups often came long distances so that they could clap, tap and chant to his marvelous music. Each friend respected the talent of the other, and they enjoyed performing together.

One day the Council of the Elders called Parray to a special meeting. He was most surprised. The young man was even more surprised once he attended the meeting, for he discovered that he had been promised in marriage to a girl from a far distant group. What's more he was expected to travel there almost immediately.

As soon as Parray heard this, he became extremely upset.

'No. No. Don't do this to me,' he protested. 'I want to marry a girl from my own group. I don't want to leave my own area.' He continued on vehemently. 'I have done nothing wrong. Why should you do this to me? Why? Why?' he demanded. It was obvious to all that he was very disturbed indeed.

The Elders were most surprised. They had expected the young man to be honored and pleased. Others would have been, but not Parray, who was becoming more agitated by the minute!

The Head Man tried to calm him by explaining that the decision was not meant to be a punishment. He went on to explain that the group who had asked

Parray to join them were in great need of a music man. In their gratitude, they were prepared to provide lots of rare, yellow ochre as well as special stones which contained beautiful blue-toned colors. Because of this everyone concerned in the negotiation, had been extremely pleased. Everyone that is, except Parray.

The Elders, in turn, assured Parray that though he would be missed by his own people he would be very much welcomed and appreciated by the new people. They felt that this would surely ease his sorrow. It did not. He faced the Elders defiantly and said, 'No. I won't go. I don't want to leave my own area and what's more I don't want to leave my friend Rurera.' He paused for a moment and then repeated, 'I won't go. I won't go.'

The Elders were astounded. Never had they witnessed such a situation. The Head Man then stood and looked hard and long at Parray. He had decided that the situation had gone far enough. In a voice that was formidable, all-powerful and stern, he said, 'It is not for you to choose.' He continued on to say, 'The Council of Elders has made the decision and you, Parray, must obey. It is not for you to choose,' he repeated, before adding, 'You will go, as directed, and what's more you will leave at dawn tomorrow! Do you understand?'

Parray felt his body go numb all over, but he nodded his head to show that he understood. He knew he would gain nothing by arguing further. As soon as he was permitted to leave the meeting he hurried to tell his friend, Rurera. As he went he wished that he had never become such a fine, sought-after musician.

That evening as darkness came upon the group and the fires were lit, the two young men were unusually quiet. It was very clear that they were both very disturbed at this turn of events.

When the evening meal had been eaten, Parray began dejectedly to gather his many didgeridoos in preparation for his journey. As he did so, he wished yet again that he had never become such a fine, sought-after musician. Then, as the people around began to settle down for the night, Parray picked up a long, thin, highly decorated instrument and began to play a special melody. It was very slow and melancholy.

A feeling of sadness came over everyone as they listened. No-one was surprised at all when Rurera began to dance. He danced in a seemingly slow-motion style, keeping to the slow, gentle, rhythm of Parray's music.

In time Parray chose another of his didgeridoos and the rhythm suddenly became quite wild. Rurera responded to the change. With tears streaming down his face he began to dance with a wild abandon which no-one had ever seen before. Somehow, the friends, in their distress at being parted, linked their minds in a somewhat crazy way. Though it was time for sleep, the dancing and the music kept on and on and on.

Rurera became like a man possessed. He danced sideways. He danced backwards. He seemed not to know what he was doing or why but still he danced. Parray meanwhile seemed to have become mesmerized by his friend's wild dancing and he played on and on.

Rurera in his dazed state danced further and further from the camp site, stepping sideways and stepping backwards as he headed towards the roaring waves of the ocean. So that his music would continue to reach his friend, Parray climbed a high tree. He managed to keep the dree-dree-dreeing of the didgeridoo coming, as he climbed to the top-most branch. All the while Rurera danced nearer and nearer to the ocean. The young man must have been totally exhausted from his hours of wild, frenzied dancing, but he still kept on.

Suddenly, a great wave rolled in from the sea and knocked him to the sand. Rurera lay there motionless as wave after wave washed over him. Within seconds the dreeing of the didgeridoo stopped and an eerie silence settled over the area.

At this time some of the people from the group ran to see why the music had ceased, but though they searched all around they could find neither of the young men. They did, however, find the didgeridoo. It was lying under the tree where it had fallen.

Several people called the young men by name, but no answer came. Some of the people began to feel a little uneasy. A strange aura of magic seemed to be heavy in the air.

Then, just as the bewildered people were about to return to their sleeping places, they spotted a strange, new, furry creature. It was a possum. It was the very first possum that had ever been seen. The bright-eyed little creature sat on a branch high up in a tree. He looked down curiously at the people and they all stared back in amazement.

Minutes later the amazed people watched as yet another strange, new creature appeared on the beach. It was a crab. It was the very first crab that had ever been seen.

Then, as the people watched in stunned silence and disbelief, the possum scrambled down from the tree, and scampered along the beach towards the side-stepping crab. The two new creatures disappeared into the darkness together.

What could it all mean?

# Beware of Willy Wagtails

*Willy wagtails feature in Aboriginal legends from many separate areas of Australia. In most legends, these feisty little birds are viewed with suspicion or else blamed for causing some form of mischief. In the Traditional period it seems they had the ability to understand and then relay human speech. Because of their 'busy body' ways they were, rightly or wrongly, usually chased out of an area as soon as they were sighted.*

BEWARE OF WILLY WAGTAILS

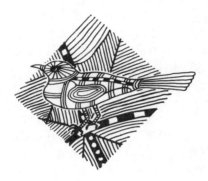

One story from the Wiradjuri people of the central west of New South Wales tells of an interesting situation which the willy wagtails created on one particular occasion. In the Wiradjuri language these chirpy little birds were known as 'dirigerees'.

This Wiradjuri story tells us that on one occasion, in the long ago, the Elders of one particular group called a rare and special meeting. It was a meeting for the men only. It was a secret meeting where the men all complained bitterly that their wives nagged them too much. This, most likely, was not true at all, but nevertheless the men decided they needed a break from their wives. With this in mind they planned a trek to visit a nearby group, and they planned to trick the women into letting them go alone.

'We'll give ourselves a few days of peace from these women,' said the Head Man. 'We will tell our wives that there is men's work to be done and we must go alone,' he added. The others all agreed.

They spent some time, then, planning their trip and most were quite excited about this chance to get away on their own. What they didn't know, however, was that there were several willy wagtails nearby.

These inquisitive little birds had listened carefully to everything that had been said. They then, of course, very quickly decided to fly over and tell the women of the group what they had heard.

'The women will be grateful and then they'll fuss over us,' said their dirigeree leader.

'Yes, they'll give us special food to eat and soft down for our nests,' added the others, excitedly. So away the willy wagtails went, making a great noise with all their bird chatter.

Just then, the women and children were having a picnic away from the camp site. They were very surprised when suddenly the friendly little birds flew down among them. The willy wagtail leader went straight up to an old lady who had special powers. He knew that she could understand his bird language. He danced and flew around the old woman for a time, loudly chirruping the story and wagging his tail all the while.

The other willy wagtails watched their leader, their excitement showing. The other women and all the children watched too. They knew that the willy wagtails were there for a reason and they could hardly wait for the old lady to translate the message. When she did translate they were, as you might expect, a little angry at what they heard. They were, however, very grateful, as the birds had expected. The women

fed the willy wagtails with their leftovers, and promised to put out more food in the days to come. In addition, they pulled fur from their kangaroo skin rugs and placed it where the birds could easily pick it up.

The willy wagtails were ecstatic. This was all very good and useful for them and they each fluttered about chirruping happily. The women, however, very quickly left the birds to themselves and organized their own secret meeting.

After an animated discussion, they decided that if the men were prepared to do without them for a few days, then these men could indeed do without them for good. 'We will leave them,' they decided, quite unanimously. They then sent one of the young women to tell the men what they had decided.

'We will create a separate camp site where we will live alone,' the young woman told the men, as she'd been instructed. 'We have chosen to do this since you don't, it seems, like having us around.' She went on to explain, 'We will no longer bother you by assisting in your hunting and gathering tasks. We will no longer grind grass seeds into flour and make hot cakes for you. We will no longer prepare hot food and drinks for you when you return from your hunts. We will no longer make rugs and cloaks of fur to keep you warm. We will no longer use our medicines and soothing oils to keep you well. We will no longer talk to you, or joke and sing with you. In future we will live alone and we expect all of you to stay away from us at all times.'

The men listened, in amazed silence. At first they were amused. Then they were astounded. Then they

were alarmed. Finally, as they realized that the girl was serious, they began to panic!

'No! No! No!' they all shouted at once. 'We want and need you all with us. We love you. Please don't leave us,' each one pleaded.

'Oh, what is this?' asked the young woman in a mocking voice. 'Can these be the same men who just a little while ago planned to get away from their terrible nagging, fussing women?'

The men looked at each other in further amazement.

'Who told you that?' asked the Head Man, very guiltily.

'That is a secret,' said the young woman with a smile as the men continued to panic.

'We really didn't mean it,' said one of the men after a time. 'We really didn't mean it. Truly!'

'That's right,' they all agreed. 'It was just a joke. We really didn't mean it.'

Eventually after much discussion between the men and the women, it was agreed that the women would not create a camp site of their own after all. It was also agreed that the men would most definitely never try to deceive them again in this way.

The men of course wondered much about it all. 'How did those women find out?' they kept asking each other.

No-one had an answer.

Meanwhile the willy wagtails chirruped happily as they lined their little nests with the fur they had been given from the kangaroo skin rugs.

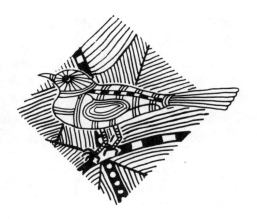

# Laugh, Kookaburra, Laugh

*The Wongaibon people, whose traditional land included the south western area of New South Wales, near to the town of Cobar, are remembered for their rare and distinctive rock paintings and also for an interesting collection of legends from the Dreaming. One particular legend explains the creation of the first kookaburra, Australia's famous laughing bird.*

In the very early days of the Dreaming, as the first people walked this land, they had much to learn and discover. Byamee, the great creator of the Wongaibon area, provided springs of water and abundant food for his people. Legends tell us however that, in this early stage, the area was in a kind of twilight zone, hazy and dark; so the people were not as happy as they could have been. They longed for more light and warmth and through their corroborees and other rituals they called upon their creator to understand their problems and help.

He did. At this time, the moon and the sun, were already functioning, but they were somewhat shrouded by mist. So Byamee cleared all the mist from the skies, so that moon and sun, each in its turn, could shine more radiantly. Byamee then planned an on-going interchange of darkness and light. He organized a set period of darkness which would be called night, and then a set period of sunlight which would be called day. And it all came to be, as planned.

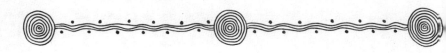

The Wongaibon people watched with pleasure as the first day dawned. Then, as the sun climbed higher into the sky, its rays became stronger and stronger. The light it gave forth was quite dazzling and the new warmth was delightful. When the people saw this they greatly rejoiced. Amazingly though, after only a few days the people began to take it all for granted. They no longer seemed to be impressed with Byamee's gift, though they enjoyed the benefits.

This surprised Byamee. He had expected that they would arise each morning, happy to rejoice with him anew. In preparation he had planned that the sunrise would be a spectacular event. For the people's pleasure he had arranged that the early morning sky would be the backdrop for an amazing art show as the delicate colors of the sun's first rays glowed brilliantly in the still dark sky. He was pleased with this early morning blend of light and shade and color, yet the people slept well into mid-morning. It seems they never knew or cared what a beautiful sight they were missing.

Because these people didn't show anywhere near the kind of joy and appreciation which he had expected, Byamee was surprised and very disappointed. Perhaps the people had become very listless while they had lived in their hazy, twilight world. Whatever the reason, their behavior was certainly hard to understand.

What could be done? Byamee wondered. Within a short while he had an interesting idea. He decided to create a rare and special bird; one which had the power to wake and also emotionally stir these seem-

ingly dull, lazy people. This he did quickly. The bird
he created was a magnificent-looking creature with
strong wings that allowed it to fly for long distances. It
had bright eyes that could spot a frog or a mouse from
a great height, and a call that was different, quite different to that of any other bird. The call was loud, raucous, echoing. It sounded for all the world like wild,
uncontrolled human laughter.

Byamee looked long at his new bird; he listened
carefully to his new bird and he was well pleased. He
named this special creature 'Kookaburra'.

As dawn was breaking the very next day he sent
the kookaburra out into the world. He sent him forth
with instructions to let his rollicking, loud laughing
call echo across the western plains till every Wongaibon
man, woman and child awoke.

The kookaburra did his job extremely well. Loud
hoots of laughter shattered the silence of the dawn and
disturbed the people as they had never been disturbed
before. It was amazing! Astounding! As his laughter
rang out in booming peals of screaming delight the
kookaburra sat high in a gum tree, watching the startled
people stumble from their sleeping places to investigate.
Early every morning after that, he began his unusual,
loud, laughing call, yet again.

Very soon, Byamee created a wife for the kookaburra, then the two sent their joined laughter echoing
strongly, joyfully for all to hear.

As expected, the people were most certainly woken,
whether they liked it or not. At first they rubbed their
eyes lazily and longed to return to bed but after a few

49

days they found that they felt better, brighter and healthier because of rising early. In addition, each began to truly appreciate the magic of daybreak; the special coolness of the breeze and the mystical, magical beauty of the sky. Very soon most of the Wongaibon people began waking early, even before hearing the exciting, happy call of the kookaburras.

Byamee was well pleased. The people even became more appreciative of all the other wonders of the world. It was like a whole new awakening for them.

As time went by the kookaburras hatched many babies which they raised carefully. Byamee taught them that it was their spirit-given duty to use their special, laughing kookaburra call to wake the world around them each morning. This they happily did.

As time went by many of these special birds traveled long distances and made their nests in new bush areas. Always though, wherever they were, they remembered what Byamee had taught them. Soon a great army of kookaburras, right across Australia, were spreading their loud, celebratory message of joy.

A great many centuries have passed since the first kookaburra was created but to this very day kookaburras have proudly and cheerfully made laughing, raucous, early morning, wake-up calls. When there is a group of them they will joyously call and answer one another, or join together to send their shrill, shrieking laughter echoing across mountains, sea and plain. Their call is one of excitement, triumph and celebration. Byamee must surely smile as he hears it. I do.

# Sacred White Clay

*Before the European colonists settled in Australia the Wiradjuri people were a large, self-sufficient, stable group. At the time of white settlement, it is estimated that they numbered more than seven thousand, probably many more. They were divided into several separate kinship-linked clans, whose camp sites were scattered across one-third of New South Wales, mainly in the central western area. In the Traditional period, more people spoke or understood the Wiradjuri language than any other native tongue.*

The Wiradjuri were a forceful, spiritual people who found all they needed in the natural resources of their area. Many legends from their Dreaming are still known and spoken of today. This is one of them.

The Wiradjuri clan, whose main camp site was by the Lachlan River (known to them as 'Kalara') in New South Wales, acknowledges the color white as being sacred. The reason for this is explained in an ancient legend about Wirroowaa, a young member of the clan who was both wise and brave. The story tells us that Wirroowaa lived in a time back in the early days of the Dreaming.

During this period, as historians and archaeologists will testify, giant kangaroos roamed this area. Some of these frightening creatures stood three metres tall. The Aboriginal people lived in constant fear of them, because, though the giants were not carnivores, they were vicious. They could and did crush the life from the defenceless people, at will.

These were the beginning, the very earliest days of Aboriginal history, and the people had not yet begun creating and using weapons of any sort. They had not begun to build shelters and fire was totally unknown to them. In this very early period, life was hazardous and somewhat difficult for them. Change was much needed.

Wirroowaa, who was desperate to help his people to make progress, asked Byamee, the great creator of that area, for help and guidance. Byamee heard the young man's plea. The creator was keen to help but needed Wirroowaa to prove his loyalty and bravery before the help could be given.

Wirroowaa vowed he would do anything that was asked of him, so Byamee commanded that he cover himself in white clay and then perform a special corroboree dance. This may seem to be an easy task but in reality it was very dangerous, very dangerous indeed, for the only white clay which was available was in the area where the giant kangaroos were camped! Wirroowaa, however, bravely accepted the challenge, and immediately began to prepare himself for the hazardous trip.

First of all, he smeared goanna oil (fat) over his whole body and then he rolled in the dust until it covered him so completely that he could hardly be distinguished from dust. He then found a very leafy branch which he held in front of himself as further camouflage. In this guise, he bravely, but very tentatively, advanced towards the giants.

As he approached the kangaroos' camp he moved very cautiously, very slowly indeed, keeping well

hidden. The kangaroos did not notice him, even though he came nearer and nearer. He was well pleased.

On arrival, he very slowly, still without attracting attention, scooped up as much clay as he could, and then quickly, but very quietly, headed back to his camp. He felt relieved and overjoyed when he reached his camp safely. He then, as instructed, carefully painted his body with the special clay. When this was done he climbed onto a high rock ledge, where he danced a lone corroboree.

His people watched and were fascinated. Byamee watched and he was well pleased. He decided, then and there, to bless the white clay, making it sacred. Then, as he had promised, Byamee began the task of improving the life of Wirroowaa's people in many, separate ways.

To begin with he caused two sticks which had been rubbing together in the breeze, to burst into flame. The flame touched the dry grass. As expected it very quickly developed into a widespread and raging fire, which grew in size and intensity by the minute. The Wiradjuri people had never seen a fire before. At first they were quite alarmed. They quickly gathered up their babies and hurried to the risen rock ledge where they felt they would be safe. They then watched in amazement and fear as the fire grew bigger still, while heat and smoke, neither of which they had experienced before, began to surround them.

From their elevated position they could see the giant kangaroos hopping wildly about. The fire was new to them, too, and it was obvious that the giant creatures

were quite terrified. As the people continued to watch, the fire seemed suddenly to take on a life-force and purpose of its own. They saw it swiftly and magically fan out to form a horse-shoe shape which totally encircled the kangaroos. The giant creatures, of course, hopped frantically towards the one available opening. At this stage, though, the fire, holding its horse-shoe shape, moved with them, so that, strange as it may seem, the fire appeared to be driving the kangaroos forward.

The kangaroos frantically bumped and banged into each other in their absolute confusion, but they each kept moving forward, heading further and further into the distance. Close behind them, the flames were leaping and roaring all the while. Eventually all the kangaroos and also the mysterious fire disappeared from view.

When this happened Wirroowaa and all of his people became very excited. It was a wonderful relief for them to realize that the giant animals were finally gone. And gone they were. The giant kangaroos were never, ever seen in that area again. However, the story does not end here.

The happy people, as you might imagine, cheered, laughed, clapped and sang as they made their way back to their camp site. It was a time of great celebration. As the excitement mounted, Wirroowaa painted the Head Man's body with the white clay, and, as expected, the clay, being blessed, had a magic effect on the old man. He found that he was instantly filled with much wisdom.

Under the power of the special white clay he was able to show his people how to make weapons. Never again

would they be in such a defenceless state. Wirroowaa
explained that weapons and other implements could be
created from many natural products including timber,
stone, bone, shell, and cord that could be made from
vines, sinew or the bark from the stringy-bark eucalypts.
He was able to suggest many varieties and introduce
different ways to make things.

The people were excited and pleased. They were all
kept busy, each one becoming part of a new production
team. Within a short time they made many spears of
different lengths and styles. They also made waddies,
shields, awls, stone axes, nets, dilly bags, millstones,
coolamons, water containers and much more. It was a
wonderfully exciting time for these early people, the first
of the Wiradjuri.

In addition the Head Man taught them how to use
fire wisely and effectively. He suggested that, whenever possible, they carry slow-burning firesticks, and
investigate ways to make fire for themselves by rubbing two sticks together. He helped them to experiment with forms of cooking, too, suggesting the use of
earth ovens and racks of coals. He also showed them
how, in the future, they could burn out large tree
trunks, as the fire had accidentally done, and then use
these as shelters.

With Byamee continuing to guide him the Head Man
was also able to discuss the building of other shelters to
keep out the rain, the wind and the sun. He showed them
how to make huts of bark and logs and leaves. Eventually
the magic of the white clay ceased but the Head Man felt
pleased that Byamee had used him in this way, even if

only for a short time. The people took note of all the Head Man had taught them. Their lifestyle, as you might expect, began to change markedly.

Not long after all of this the Head Man who was very old, grew weak and died. Wirroowaa, as expected, became the new leader. He and his people remembered and did everything that the old man had said and their lives became much easier from that time on.

As the centuries passed, this clan of the Wiradjuri, and all the others, too, progressed and grew in number. Down through the ages each new generation of people continued the practice of painting their bodies with white clay before a corroboree or a special ceremony. This was to show that they remembered Byamee their creator and appreciated his special on-going interest in them, at all times.

The people of that early time told the story of the sacred white clay to their children. It has continued to be told to each new generation of Wiradjuri people, generation after generation, for centuries. It was told to me as I grew up in Wiradjuri territory in the second half of this century.

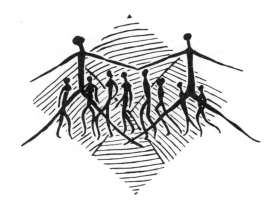

# The Whale's Canoe

*There are many legends which tell of the creation
of the birds, the animals and the first people of
Australia. One from Wiradjuri territory in central
western New South Wales, presents a very
interesting view. It is said that Byamee, the great
creator of that area, told this story himself to one
particularly privileged group. It explains that in
the very early period, a period before the Dreaming
began, there were very few people and very little
wildlife at all. Australia then, was a quiet paradise
of beautiful trees, wide rivers and peaceful
landscapes. It was a large, sun-drenched island
waiting quietly for its destiny to be fulfilled.*

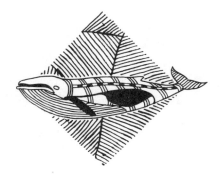

During the very early days of Australia's Dreaming, there were very few birds and animals in the land. Across the sea, to the north, there were many different species of birds and animals. There were too many in fact. They were all crowded together and wished desperately for more space. Some of the birds from the land to the north were able to fly away and settle in the lovely, sparsely inhabited land to the south; but the other creatures were not so fortunate. One particular group of them longed to make a migratory trip, and they discussed the possibility over and over again.

In those early days, of course, before things were as they are now, the animals, the birds, and the creatures of the sea could all communicate with each other. It was a very exciting period in history.

These particular creatures had their hearts and minds set most definitely on journeying to the great south land but, despite all their discussions, there seemed no way that they could manage it. A few of

them had frail canoes which they offered for use but each was found to be totally unsuitable.

What could they do? The whale was the only one who had a sufficiently large and strong canoe, but, though he used it very rarely, he refused to lend it at any time, for any reason. He was by nature a very selfish and mean creature and he guarded his canoe well, keeping it by his side at all times.

Eventually the desperate group sent the emu and the kangaroo to beg him to change his mind. This they did, without success. Though they promised to do many favors for the whale in return for the use of his canoe, and though they pointed out that he could easily retrieve it from the great south land when their journey was done, the whale was not interested.

'No,' he shouted, over and over again. 'No, no, a thousand times no! I will never lend you my canoe.' He then laughed at them mockingly before yelling 'Go away you stupid, foolish creatures. Go away and don't come near me or my canoe ever again!'

When the emu and the kangaroo reported this conversation to the members of their group they were all terribly disappointed. These creatures wanted so very much to get to the beautiful south land and now their only chance seemed to be gone.

The little starfish, who was a very kindly creature, saw that they were most unhappy and he felt sorry for them. He was one of the few creatures who had ever shared any sort of a friendship with the whale, but on this occasion even he felt that the whale had been unnecessarily mean. The starfish had long been

recognized as a clever storyteller. In the past he had often sat on the whale's head while telling his stories. The starfish always enjoyed this as he got an exciting ride, and, in addition, the stories had seemed to please and quieten the usually mean old whale, who would close his eyes and relax as he listened.

After much thought the little starfish decided to use his storytelling talent to trick the whale. We know, of course, that it is never good to deceive anyone, not even a mean old whale, but on this occasion the starfish felt it was somehow justified. The starfish decided to tell to the whale that evening the best of all his stories. He then suggested to the members of the special group that they each swim out, climb quietly into the whale's canoe and then row away, while the giant creature listened, with his eyes firmly closed. It was a risky plan because the giant was capable of destroying every single one of them if their plot was discovered! However, the members of this determined little group were very keen to get to their dream island, so they each bravely decided to give the plan a go.

That evening, true to his word, the helpful little starfish climbed upon the great whale's head and began to tell a very special story. The story was indeed exciting. As expected, the whale soon closed his eyes, letting his mind relax, while the starfish went on and on with the story. Meanwhile, as planned, the other creatures swam out to the whale's canoe. As quietly as possible they scrambled aboard. Quickly, and in a very excited state, they pulled back the oars and headed southward.

The starfish watched them go as he bravely continued on with his story. Just as the canoe disappeared from view, the whale called out: 'Is my canoe safe?'

'Yes, yes,' answered the little starfish nervously. 'Listen and I'll tap against it for you.' The little creature then tapped two pieces of wood together making it sound as if he had tapped the side of the canoe. The whale heard the sound. He was somehow convinced that all was well and he relaxed even more as the starfish continued with his story. The starfish felt somewhat guilty for tricking his friend in this way but he kept telling himself that the whale would eventually recover his canoe again and so, no harm would be done. How wrong he was!

When the little starfish was satisfied that the canoe and its passengers were safely out of sight and out of danger, he finished his story. At this point he planned to slither quickly off the whale's head and then explain what he had done, before suggesting that the whale swim southward and calmly retrieve his canoe. As stated, the starfish planned to explain it all but he didn't get a chance.

As soon as the whale opened his eyes he saw that his precious canoe was gone and he knew that he had been tricked. He instinctively knew who was in his canoe and where it was heading. Instantly, he became extremely angry. He did not wait for an explanation. He did not want one. Without warning he savagely flipped the starfish into the air, then caught him in his giant jaws. He shook the little creature quite violently before spitting him out. Though the starfish was still

alive, he found his whole body had been turned to jelly. And that is how it was to stay forever.

It seems too that the starfish, having perched on the whale's head for so long on this occasion, had left a hole there and this, too, was to stay forever. However, the whale was in no mood to worry about the strange, new hole in his head. He very quickly headed southward in search of his canoe. He was in a terrible rage and his giant body sped through the water extremely quickly and forcefully. In a few hours he sighted the overloaded vessel. The escaping birds and animals, with a koala doing most of the rowing, were heading into shore on the eastern coast of the great south land. The whale surged towards the canoe in a frenzy of rage. How dare they take his canoe? How dare they?

When he reached the canoe he savagely upturned it and the kangaroo, the koala, the emu, the brolga, the wombat, the echidna and the others were all tossed into the surging sea. They all splashed about frantically until they got their bearings. Then they each swam for their lives towards the shore. Somehow, amazingly, they all managed to reach it safely.

As each one in turn scrambled onto the beach they watched as the upturned canoe split into pieces. They were amazed as they watched, for the broken pieces reformed and magically became a little off-shore island. The whale was more angry than ever when this happened and he shouted terrible threats at the half-drowned group. He was doubly angry now for he realized that in his rage he had actually destroyed his

own canoe. The travelers watched him from the safety of the sand, and in time the whale, still in a rage, headed out to sea.

The animals looked around their new area and were quietly delighted. Without waiting any longer they each headed off to find their own special place in this new and exciting land. Almost all of them decided to settle quite a distance from the coast because none of them wanted to meet with the whale ever again. In time each animal had its own family and they all lived very happily, just as they had expected, in the beautiful, lush, south land to which they had come.

Byamee, the creator of the area where they settled, was pleased to see that they had come to share his land. From that time on he guarded and watched over them all as if they were his own. Soon the animals and their offspring were all very much a part of this wide, brown land. And the whale, who decided never to get so angry again, was often seen swimming around the little island that had once been his canoe.

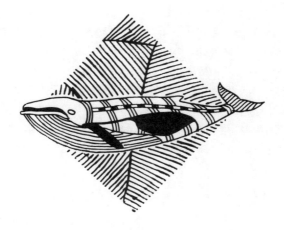

# How the Turtle Came to Be

*There is a legend which comes from the coastal
area of Queensland, just a little north of where
Brisbane is today. It comes from the Mooloola
people. It is the story of an Aboriginal man who
lived in the early days of the Dreaming, a man
who had exceptional ability in story telling and the
making of music.*

This is the story of Mungi. He lived many centuries ago when the Dreaming was still quite new. He belonged to no particular group. It was his task to travel throughout the northern region, telling to each of the groups the stories of their beginnings and the work which had been done by their ancestor spirits. He enchanted all the people still more by making didgeridoo music as well as singing and chanting, the like of which had never been heard before. He spent time too in teaching the people of each group to follow his example by expressing their own joy, appreciation and even their fear through music and chanting.

Mungi loved his job. He delighted in telling stories and entertaining people with his music. He also enjoyed being constantly on the move. Whenever he was coaxed to stay more than a few weeks with any one group he would find himself getting very restless. It seemed that a force within him compelled him to constantly travel, to keep moving on.

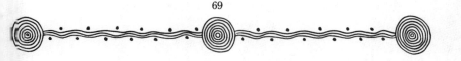

There came a time when Mungi was invited to visit a small group who had years earlier made camp on an island, a short distance from shore. Mungi was interested but was forced to refuse, initially, because he had never learned to swim. At this point, two of the group's strongest hunters, both of whom were also excellent swimmers, offered to hold him up between them as they glided through the water. Mungi agreed and they ferried him safely, in this manner, across the sea to the island camp. The people there welcomed him happily. They provided him with special foods and made him a soft, safe bed in which to sleep each night. Mungi, as expected, told his wonderful stories, played his didgeridoo, tapped his cleverly designed tap-sticks together and sang and chanted song after song.

Several weeks passed and eventually Mungi — though he had enjoyed his stay immensely — suggested that the time had come for him to leave.

'Please stay,' all the people begged.

'If you stay a little longer,' said the two strong hunters 'we will teach you how to swim.' Mungi wanted very badly to learn to swim, so he decided to stay a while longer.

He waited for several days, continuing to tell stories and entertain the people, but the hunters did not come forth to teach him to swim. Mungi gradually came to understand that they had tricked him. He considered the problem for some time and then decided that he would attempt to wade back to the mainland. He had convinced himself that he could manage somehow to keep his head above the water.

As planned, Mungi bravely set out, but, of course, the water was far deeper than he had imagined. Very soon, as you might expect, he was in terrible trouble. He would have drowned, without doubt, except that the two strong hunters saw him struggling in the water and swam out to save him. They saved him; but they were both very angry.

'If you try to leave us again,' they said meanly, 'we will spear you!'

This shocked Mungi. Once he was safely back at the island camp he made no mention of their frightening threat, but he did not forget it. He quickly organized himself and began once again to chant his songs and create his marvelous music. It seemed to those around him that Mungi was his usual happy self once again, but he most certainly was not! Mungi was desperately unhappy and in time he devised a clever escape plan which he felt sure would work.

The following night, as part of his plan, he played his didgeridoo and tapped his tap-sticks in an especially wild, exciting rhythm. The people loved it. Before the evening was through, however, he made sure, as part of his escape plan, that he had broken every single one of his special tap-sticks. The people from the group, offered to make new ones but Mungi simply shook his head. He told them that his tap-sticks could only be cut from a large hollow hardwood log, the like of which could only be found on the mainland.

The people could not quite understand why this should be so, but eventually, the two strong hunters were dispatched to find such a log. This they did, though they

were angry at being ordered to go. As soon as they had floated the log back to their island, they urged Mungi to cut his tap-sticks from it. He refused. He told them, as a further part of his plan, that he must first carve a special pattern on the log. This pattern had to be left undisturbed all through the night. The hunters, and the other people of the group, found this, also, hard to understand. Yet again they decided to let him have his way.

Late that night, when every person in the camp was fast asleep, Mungi, as he had planned all along, quietly pushed the patterned log to the water's edge. He then pulled himself into the hollowed-out section of the log and let it float away across the sea. The log headed, as he had hoped, towards the mainland shore and he propelled it, as best he could, with his arms and legs.

He had not manoeuvred the log very far before the two hunters awoke. They, of course, looked across the water, saw the floating log, and realized immediately what had happened. Instantly they grabbed their spears, took aim and threw them one after another at the log and Mungi. But Mungi had anticipated this. He pulled his arms, head and legs into the log. As expected, he found he was safe. The spears all struck the outside of the log. None could penetrate the solid hardwood. Mungi, very happily, proceeded on his way, delighted that his plan had worked thus far.

After a time, however, he put his head out to see if he were drawing near to the shore. This was indeed a foolish move for the hunters were still watching from afar. With the speed of lightning, one of them threw yet another spear. The spear struck Mungi in the neck.

With a cry he fell face down into the water and it seemed as if he would surely die.

But his ancestor spirits were watching. They did not think it right that he should die so they decided to use their special powers. Through their magic they saved his life, but from that moment, Mungi's human form was completely changed. When he finally reached safety, Mungi clambered onto the sandy shore. There he found that he had become a new creature, an amphibious creature which would wear for all time to come, a protective shell on its back.

Mungi had become a turtle, the very first one. He quickly realized that he would no longer be able to sing and entertain his people. Though this made him sad, he was pleased to be alive and pleased that even as a turtle he could continue to travel from place to place, peacefully, through all the days of his life.

# The Message of the Butterflies

*This legend comes from the Barkindji people of northern New South Wales. It is thought-provoking; a legend you will not easily forget. It explains how the very first Barkindji people came to understand and accept death. It explains how they came to an awakening belief in life beyond the grave.*

There was a time when the creation of this land was still very, very new; when the birds and animals and all other creatures shared a common language; when humans could interchange their form or personality with that of birds and animals; when the concept of death and dying was still unknown. This was in the early days of the Dreaming. As you might expect, however, a death did eventually occur.

One evening a young cockatoo fell from its nest and lay lifeless on the ground with its neck broken. The first people, together with all the other birds and creatures, were very concerned, and indeed quite frightened. This was something they had no concept of; they did not understand.

A great crowd stood around silently and watched as the humans tried, unsuccessfully, to revive the bird. After a time the Elders of the group decided that the ever-present spirits must have chosen to take the life force from the cockatoo so that it could be transformed

or used in some new way. Still, they were very puzzled by this new occurrence. They agreed that they needed to experiment further.

They called for volunteers. At first no-one at all was keen to die so that the process could be studied by the others, but after a time some lowly caterpillars did, tentatively, offer their services. It was understood that the phenomenon of death, as seen by what had happened to the cockatoo, meant that those creatures involved in the experiment had to reach a stage in which they were totally still. They had to reach a stage in which they did not move, eat, see, hear, or do anything at all. It was agreed that the caterpillars must somehow mesmerize themselves into such a state and then maintain it for a period of time, to see what would happen.

A protective cocoon was duly made for each caterpillar. The cocoons were attached to the limbs of the tallest trees, some of which almost reached up to the sky-world. All through the long, cold winter the cocoons hung there in that place. At first the eager people watched them with great anticipation. But days and weeks went by and there was no change, no magic transformation, nothing at all to see. The people of course became very disappointed. Meanwhile, they kept themselves very busy making tools, gathering food, learning to build shelters and generally helping each other. Indeed they were so busy that, as the winter months slowly passed, most of them quite forgot about the caterpillars who had crawled into those dark cocoons, so many weeks earlier.

During this beginning period in time, the pattern of the four seasons was also still developing. The people were pleased indeed when, after the long, cold, bleak winter, the earth gradually began to warm up, yet again. They were delighted. It was exciting to see the buds bursting into blossoms; to see the leaves growing again on the bare trees; and most of all to feel the sun becoming warmer and warmer each day.

The people were so pleased that they began planning a feast and a special corroboree of celebration. They wished, through their corroboree, to show their gratitude to their creator for all the joys of the new season which we now know as spring. The celebration feast had just begun when a whole bunch of excited dragonflies swarmed in among the people.

'Look up. Look up,' they urged. 'Look up at the cocoons. They are splitting open!'

A breathless hush fell upon the crowd as all eyes turned expectantly towards the tall trees. Each person gasped in amazement and wonder as, one after another, the cocoons opened, letting loose a host of beautiful butterflies, the like of which had never been seen before. The delicate creatures fluttered gently down to be admired. They spread their fragile, multi-colored wings, the colors of which shone radiantly, iridescently, in the soft light. They rested gracefully on nearby bushes and trees. They looked splendid.

All the people watched in quiet delight. They were pleased that their experiment had been successful. The dull, ordinary caterpillars had indeed been magically and wonderfully transformed. It was a most exciting

result and the people, after that, lost their fear of death.

After such a demonstration, they would always see the process of death as a stage, as a still and silent stage, prior to a wondrous and exciting transformation, a new beginning.

Now, centuries have passed, and generation after generation of Aboriginal people have been born and have lived out their lives in this area. And all of them, together with most other people from other areas, have continued to hold this belief firmly in their hearts. Their faith has been renewed every spring as yet another cluster of beautiful butterflies has magically emerged.

# The Star Sisters

*The Aboriginal people of all areas had a deep knowledge of the visible stars. They understood the changing phases of the moon and the seasonal effects of the sun. This knowledge was deeply etched into the consciousness of all and helped to form the social and cultural pattern of their lives. There are a vast number of legends and stories to explain the changing pattern of the sky and the mystery of the stars.*

The legend of the Star Sisters was well known by the groups who lived in the north eastern section of South Australia, during the Traditional period. It is a legend about the Pleiades. The Pleiades has aroused interest and speculation in all lands, through all eras of time. In contemporary Western society this group of stars is generally referred to as 'The Seven Sisters'. This has come from the classic Greek legend which tells how the seven daughters of Atlas and Pleione were transformed into stars by the Gods of that long-ago era.

Within the Aboriginal realm there are several separate beliefs. The people of some Traditional groups believed that the Pleiades stars were the shining leaves of six or seven gum trees, placed there by ancestor spirits to give shade and shelter to the dead as they made their lone journey into the spirit world. Legends from other areas tell us that the stars represent a group of white kangaroos which are being chased eternally by wild dingos from the constellation of Orion. There

are others which tell us that the stars are the children of a favored Head Man who now lives there in the sky-world. Still others, as in Greek mythology, refer to the stars as being a group of sisters.

The three Aboriginal groups who shared the north eastern part of South Australia are among those who saw the stars as sisters. They believed them to be human sisters who had once lived in their area. They believed that the sisters in years long past had been wooed by, then married to, men from the great Orion constellation. The sisters, who were thought to be living happily in the sky-world, were said to be extremely beautiful and had remained eternally young. They were unusually fair with long free-flowing, silver-colored hair and their pale bodies were covered by glistening icicles.

As all star gazers know the Pleiades disappears over the western horizon about one hour ahead of the Orion constellation. This occurs, we are told, because the sisters, as affectionate, loyal wives, go ahead of their men to prepare the cooking fires etc. When their husbands, the Orion hunters, reach them, after journeying across the sky, the evening meal is cooked, then enjoyed, away from the gaze of the earth people.

During the cold winter months, when the stars of the Pleiades are most clearly seen in South Australia, the sisters remember their earthly people. In an effort to share their sky-world magic of beauty and youth they brush the frozen icicles from their bodies and let them fall silently to the earth below. The icicles form a frost on the ground, but it remains only for a short time. It disappears as soon as the rays of the rising sun touch it.

In the Traditional period, the teenage girls and boys of that area made a ritual of rubbing the pre-dawn frost over their bodies believing that its magical qualities would help them to grow up to be strong, healthy and above all, attractive.

It is not known if this custom is still practised today.

# Kulia and the Sea Creature

*This legend of Kulia and Culma, the sea creature, comes from the coastal area of the Gulf of Carpentaria. It was first told by the Goonanderry people. It was told to each new generation of their children as they grew up there in the long ago. It was told as a warning.*

This is the story of a very young echidna who was called Kulia. Though he was old enough to amble about in the bush he was still young enough to live with and be protected by his parents. His parents guarded him well. Over and over again they warned him of the dangers of the nearby ocean.

'You must never, ever go near to the sea,' they said. 'The sea is no place for an echidna. You are a bush creature.' Little Kulia listened obediently and promised, over and over again, that he would never, ever go near the sea!

One day while the mother and father echidna were busy fossicking for food, Kulia became bored, and he decided to go looking for adventure. He walked in his bumbly way in one direction, then another. He didn't have any idea where he was heading, but he kept shuffling along, anyway. Eventually he found himself on the soft sand of the nearby beach. He loved the feel of the sand under his little feet, and he loved the look of the surging sea.

'This is lots of fun,' he thought, 'and it seems very safe and quiet.' Somewhere in the back of his mind he remembered that his parents had told him, over and over again, that he must never, ever go near the waters of the sea. He remembered but, like most other children, he pushed the thought out of his mind. He decided that just once he wanted to feel the wetness of the sea on his hot little feet. Could this be so bad?

'I'll just splash around for a little bit and then I'll hurry home,' said he to himself. Oh how foolish he was!

Suddenly he realized that he was not alone. A soft whitish-grey sea creature had sidled up to have a chat with him.

'Who are you?' asked the seemingly gentle sea creature in an ever-so-friendly voice. Kulia was not afraid at all and proudly told the creature his echidna name.

'Will you come for a swim with me?' asked the sea creature in its gentle, whining voice.

'I'd like to but I can't,' answered Kulia. 'You see I don't know how to swim.'

'That is not a problem,' said the whitish-grey creature. 'There is plenty of sand for non-swimmers to stand upon,' it added, smiling sweetly all the while.

We know, of course, that this was not true, but Kulia did not understand that there were bad creatures as well as good creatures in this world! He believed what he heard and consequently decided to venture a little further into the big, wide, cooling sea. He felt the water gradually covering most of his little body. It felt really good.

His large, whitish-grey friend kept saying, 'Come on. Come on little one. Come just a little further.' So he did, though he was becoming a little nervous. Just as he began to say, 'No. I think this is far enough,' his feet lost touch with the sand. Within seconds he found himself completely swamped. He began to splutter and choke.

Poor little Kulia gulped and struggled. He looked frantically toward his new friend for help but the soft, whitish-grey sea creature looked at him, meanly, as it said, 'Aah ha! Aah ha! I've got you now little bush creature. Aah ha ha!'

Kulia realized, too late, that he had been tricked. Oh, how he wished then, that he had heeded his mother and father. He frantically rolled himself into a little ball, hoping somehow, that the waves might even yet wash him safely to shore. They didn't. The sly, whitish-grey creature slowly opened its great mouth. Then it swallowed the unfortunate little echidna in one almighty gulp. Oh dear!

Later that day the mother and father echidna hurried back to their safe little nest. They had food for their baby but no matter how they searched they could not find him. We know why!

The big whitish-grey sea creature did not go entirely unpunished. As Kulia was being swallowed he bravely stuck out his sharp little echidna spikes. They pierced the body of the big sea creature making it look spiky too. To this day, these whitish-grey creatures still swim in the tropical waters of the Gulf of Carpentaria; and to this day they still have a very spiky fin and tail.

# The Legend of Black Mountain

*In Cooktown, northern Queensland, the legend of Black Mountain is very well known and retold quite often. The mountain which is spoken of in the legend is comprised entirely of stark, bare, black boulders. It rises to a height of more than four hundred metres and stretches more than four kilometres in width. It is indeed a strange and sinister seeming, geographic feature. The Black Mountain can be seen, towering above the lush tropical rainforest, a short distance south of the gold-mining township of Cooktown.*

The mountain has long been regarded by locals as a mysterious place, a place of tragedy. In recent times several persons have disappeared while attempting to climb it; no vegetation grows on the slopes; birds and animals avoid it and most people, Aboriginal and non Aboriginal, would not wish to walk upon it.

The legend of Black Mountain is short and straightforward. It is said that, at one stage during the Dreaming era, there was no mountain. There were black boulders of varying sizes scattered across the plain, but no mountain. In its place there was a fertile area where animals abounded and wild berries and grasses flourished. At this time, among the group who lived nearby were two brothers, Tajalruji and Kalruji. They were fine respected hunters. Both brothers, like their totem animal the wallaby, were active, agile, quick and strong.

The two were the main gatherers of food for their people, providing a large proportion of the meat required. They always hunted as a team. From the time that they

were both very young the two had understood and supported each other extremely well. They were very close indeed.

One day, while both young men were absent from their own camp site, they came upon a beautiful girl. She was alone. She was digging for yams. They stood for a time, watching her graceful movements as she worked. They knew from markings on her yam stick that she belonged to a neighboring group whose totem was the rock python.

A wife had already been chosen for each of the brothers but both Tajalruji and Kalruji knew in an instant that they wanted this girl instead. Because the rock python group was one of the groups their wallaby group were allowed to marry, each young man knew that, though another had been promised, it was not entirely impossible for one of them to get this girl as his wife. Each brother began secretly to plan for this. The lovely girl looked up and smiled at them both as they passed.

As soon as they were at a distance from the girl each declared his plan to the other. They then, of course, began to argue. This was unfortunate for never before had the two quarreled. Each brother was determined to win the argument, and also the girl. Each became more angry by the minute.

Eventually it was decided that they must force the issue and fight, fight until one brother were vanquished and one victorious. This was difficult because their tribal law forbade any hunters within the group to use their weapons against each other. How could they solve their problem?

After several hours of argument they agreed upon an unusual contest. They agreed that each would build a tower, using the black boulders. It was jointly decided that whoever had the highest tower, when their labors finally ceased, would win the chance to marry the girl.

The girl watched and listened to this decision, quietly, from a distance. She continued to watch with great interest as they both began to build. It was difficult for each man to lift the boulders but somehow they managed it. They toiled all through that day, and then through the next as well. Both towers gradually rose higher and higher. By the third day news about the contest had spread and people from both the wallaby totem group and the rock python group came to watch. The watchers expected the young men to faint with exhaustion at any moment because neither of them had slept for three days. Somehow, though, both continued to labor. After three days of constant stacking and piling, both towers had become quite enormous.

The girl had come each day to watch the two young men toiling feverishly on. By the third day she was totally amazed and wondered much about the final result. The ever-growing crowd of spectators had also begun to speculate on the outcome. Some among them thought that Tajalruji would win; others were just as sure that Kalruji, being younger, would build the tallest tower. At different times during the incredible three-day effort one brother would appear to be winning. Then a boulder would topple from his tower — or the other brother would manage to place yet another rock. At no stage was it clear who would be the victor.

As the fourth day dawned clouds began to form in the sky and a fierce wind began to blow. Both young men continued to toil on, regardless. The girl noticed that a storm was coming but she was too intrigued by the situation to leave the scene. The spectators had become so keenly interested in the bitter contest that most of them didn't even notice the approaching storm.

Then suddenly, in mid afternoon it struck. There was a deafening thunderclap; lightning flashed across the plain. Then, to the surprise of all, rain began to fall more heavily than it had ever done before. Instinctively the people of both groups ran towards the two massive, jagged towers in search of shelter.

As they ran the people watched in horror as the wild wind scooped up both Tajalruji and Kalruji and sent them hurtling, as if they were toys, from the top of their towers. Both young men were carried up, up, out of sight, beyond the clouds. The vicious wind then lifted the frightened girl off her feet dashing her body against the black boulders before she too was carried up and into the sky-world.

As time went by the wind became even more intense and very soon all the black boulders that had been so carefully stacked were being tossed about the sky like marbles. The terrified people ran this way and that, screaming all the time for their ancestor spirits to protect them. No help came.

Perhaps the ancestor spirits were disappointed because the brothers had chosen to ignore their sacred marriage ties. Perhaps they were disappointed because

so much time and energy had been wasted on such a seemingly trivial endeavor. No-one knows, but the ancestor spirits, for their own reasons, allowed the storm to roar and rage on, becoming more fierce and terrifying by the minute. Gradually, one by one, the spectators were either battered to death or completely crushed by the falling boulders. No-one escaped.

By the time the ferocious wind had blown itself out and the rain had ceased to fall, both the enormous towers had disappeared. Every one of the black boulders, both the large and the small, had been hurtled about the sky then tossed together into one huge, massive, tangled heap. Thrown together they had formed a mighty and jagged mountain, a vast, totally sombre, black mountain, made of solid rock. The bodies of the people who had lost their lives in the terrible storm were never recovered. Though this happened many centuries ago a frightening and very real feeling of 'disquiet' has continued to hover around this place.

To this day, the mysterious mountain still stands there, forebodingly. Not surprisingly, it is now officially known as Black Mountain. The feeling of disquiet has continued. Few people venture near the mountain. The only living creatures that feel at ease on its slopes are the totem animals of those two Aboriginal groups, the agile black wallaby and the unobtrusive rock python.

# Fire Magic

*There is a large collection of legends concerning the acquisition of fire and its subsequent uses. The content of these stories varies from group to group. In some areas stories of the first fire have deep spiritual connections, while in other areas the stories were told simply to entertain the people as they rested at the end of the day. One ancient and much favored legend comes from the Ngulugwongga people of Northern Australia whose traditional land included the area where Darwin, Northern Territory, now stands. The legend is well known and is often retold by Ngulugwongga descendants, today. It tells of the practice of creating fire by using friction, a process used by Traditional Aboriginal people of Australia.*

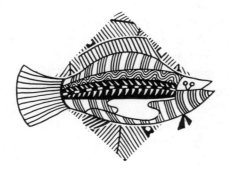

This is the story of Numal, a Ngulugwongga magic man who lived in the very early days of creation, back in a time when humans, animals, birds and sea creatures could interchange bodies and communicate with each other. Numal, through his mysterious links with the spirit world, had been blessed with the gift of fire. At this point in time he was the only human who had been blessed in this way. He carried his precious fire in the form of a special slow-burning firestick which he kept close by at all times. He used it to start a large fire each time his people made a new camp. The fires provided light and warmth and of course, through the process of cooking, made their food more appetizing. His people knew that they were extremely privileged and they felt very honored and very grateful to him.

Numal was a kind-hearted man who was pleased to be of service to his people and also to others. Whenever his people met another group he would patiently reveal the many benefits of fire before sharing with them the

burning coal from his firestick. The others were always most grateful. As you might expect, as time passed, news of the firestick spread to groups far distant. Scouts from these came to inquire about and share the wondrous gift. Numal was always willing to help and these travelers always went away, well pleased. Often they would leave gifts or a promise of a favor to come, to show their gratitude. It was a peaceful time of caring, sharing, and helpful communication.

The time came, however, when this pleasant situation was altered. The change began when a man of the fish people, who lived in the sea, came to visit. He had changed himself into a human for the purpose of the visit. (In those days, this was possible.) Unbeknown to the Ngulugwongga people, this man was an evil creature who had come to steal Numal's special firestick. The sea creature didn't want to simply *share* in the secret of fire. He wanted to *own* it and totally control it. He wanted power over both the land and the sea and he felt that Numal's firestick would get it for him.

The fish man, of course, pretended great friendship and the unsuspecting Ngulugwongga people made him welcome, as was their custom. After the evening meal the people settled down to sleep and the visitor watched carefully as Numal stored his precious firestick in hot ashes by the campfire.

'The use of fire is of great benefit to your people,' said the fish man, hoping to get Numal talking and so learn a little more about it, before he stole the stick.

'It is indeed,' answered Numal. 'But sadly it is of no use to your people. It is of no use at all, for you are of

the sea and my fire will not burn in your realm.'

The fish man heard this but he refused to believe it, would not even consider that it might be true. 'What nonsense,' he thought. He then became even more determined to steal the firestick.

Hours of darkness passed and when he was sure that all of the people were sound asleep he quietly picked up the precious firestick. Then, holding it carefully, he stealthily headed towards his home, the sea. As he reached the water's edge the firestick was splashed by incoming waves. Immediately smoke began to rise and the hot coals steamed and sizzled in a desperate effort to avoid being doused. The sea creature saw that there was a problem so he lifted the firestick higher as he waded deeper into the water. He was still stubbornly determined, however, somehow to make the firestick flare and flame anew in the depths of his watery world.

Numal, meanwhile, had awoken and realized what had happened. Led by the light of his magic firestick he had silently followed the fish man to the shore. He was now watching in horror as the evil creature waded deeper and deeper into the water. Numal knew that the magic power of his firestick would be lost forever once it was covered by water so he made a desperate and quite amazing dash to catch up with the fish man.

Somehow he managed it and the two began to fight savagely. Numal had never before had to fight but he was extremely strong. He was also very determined to save his firestick so eventually he won. The sea creature then changed back to being a fish and angrily dived deep into the sea while Numal grasped the firestick anxiously. He

then staggered, exhausted, onto the shore. When he was completely clear of the waves and their spray he sat alone on the sand, deeply in thought. He was very troubled.

This incident had made him realize that there was evil in this new world. He knew that in time some other sea creature, or perhaps a power-hungry land person, would attempt yet again to steal his firestick. And what if they succeeded? Its wonderful magic could be lost forever, or worse still, it could be used in a destructive way.

Numal knew that he must somehow guard against this. It seemed that the only solution was to break up the precious firestick, spreading and sharing the magic sparks. If this happened no one person could ever gain control. He realized that to manage this he would have to travel throughout this newly created land and leave a share of the magic in each separate area. He decided he would do it. He would leave sparks hidden, in each area, then give instructions on how to release the fire magic when needed.

The very next day Numal valiantly set off on his long, lone journey. He travelled for many seasons across many mountains, many valleys, many rivers and many plains. He travelled north, west, east and south. In each new area he followed a carefully planned routine. Firstly, he selected a special tree. He then beat his special firestick against the tree making sure that several sparks flew up and settled in the branches. The sparks were then left to lie there, dormant and hidden, protected by spirit-given magic, until the men of that group sought and released

the flames. Numal showed them how to do this by rubbing together two twigs from the tree.

The years slowly passed by and Numal grew tired and very old, but he kept on until he had visited each separate area in the land. Eventually he returned to his beloved Ngulugwongga people and his northern area homeland. There he died. He had successfully shared the blessing of fire, the blessing which had been entrusted to him by the spirits. He felt that his ancestor spirits would be well pleased with him. And they were.

As the centuries passed Numal's secret of creating fire, by rubbing two special sticks together, was carefully passed down from one generation to the next. This happened in each and every Aboriginal camp site right across the land.

Numal of the Ngulugwongga people lived in the very early days of Aboriginal history when the Dreaming had just begun, but he is still remembered today. His gift of fire has been appreciated through tens of thousands of years and many corroborees have been danced in his honor.

# The Rainbow Serpent

*Legends concerning the great Rainbow Serpent are among those which were, and have continued to be, the most widespread of all the Aboriginal legends. They come from all groups and all areas across Australia.*

From a study of many legends from all parts of the continent we learn that the Rainbow Serpent was a magnificent creature, beautifully multi-colored. It was as large as a dinosaur with the will and super intelligence of a god-like being. It is said that the Rainbow Serpent appeared during the mysterious Dreaming time. The land was quite flat at that time but, as the steadily writhing body of the giant serpent slid from place to place, deep gorges, rivers, mountains and valleys in the shape of its body were formed.

Through the legends we learn that the Rainbow Serpent was prepared to devote its life to the care and protection of all Aboriginal people and it was understood that its spirit would continue to live on indefinitely in the dark depths of certain waterholes. It was accepted that the Serpent would always watch the affairs of Aboriginal people, and would in all circumstances be prepared to guard and guide them. The magnificent Rainbow Serpent was thought of as being totally sacred.

In Traditional times Aboriginal people of all groups paid homage to this great being of their past in that, among their most highly prized possessions, were decorated, ancient stones which they accepted as being the Serpent's eggs. These were stored in a secret, sacred place and were shown only during special ceremonies, such as an initiation. Each stone was carefully passed down from generation to generation and was much revered.

In a few areas there was a belief that the great Rainbow Serpent actually gave life to all. The legends from these areas tell us that the giant Serpent went about the land producing many babies some of which grew to be the first men and women, while others became the first animals and birds. The Rainbow Serpent provided springs of fresh water, as well as food and shelter, in these areas, so that all of its offspring would prosper.

In all areas, whenever a rainbow was seen arched across the sky, it was thought of as a symbol or a reflection of the magical, mighty creature, and looked upon with wonder. Many special corroborees were created and danced in its honor. The giant Rainbow Serpent, whose splendid image was drawn in the sand, cut into the moss of rocks, chipped into sandstone chunks and painted on bark and in caves all across this land, was regarded with awe by generations of Aboriginal people.

Even today its existence is shrouded in mystery and spoken of with great respect.

# Manindi — A Special Dingo

*In the Traditional period each of the groups regarded one or more colors as being sacred. Several groups from inland Australia, in the area where the New South Wales and South Australian borders meet, considered red to be significant to their area. These included the Ngauri and the Piladapa people. Body painting, in preparation for all ritual and also most social ceremonies revealed a dominance of red. It was also evident in their rock paintings and in the decoration of their implements. The coloring was ocher based. In this area there was a huge supply of this very rare, richly red clay. The people used it extensively within their own groups. They also gained much from bartering the clay to other groups, some far distant. A legend from this area tells why the surrounding plains produced a seemingly unlimited supply of special, red-toned ocher.*

In the early days of Aboriginal history, a giant lizard, one of dinosaur proportions, lived in the Flinders Ranges and preyed upon the unfortunate people. Many brave hunters attempted to protect their people but nothing seemed to baulk or worry the massive creature.

At this time the Ngauri people had a pet dingo which they had named Manindi. They had found Manindi as a pup and raised him. Though he now roamed free, he remained their faithful friend.

One day the giant, marauding lizard approached a peaceful camp site, planning yet again to drag away some of the defenceless people. Manindi saw the beast approaching. He was afraid, but he steeled himself to fight to the death to save the people. Manindi walked to the edge of the camp site and attacked the surprised lizard. He was no match in size for the giant but he was very ferocious and very determined to defend his people.

The battle raged for several hours and the people

watched in horror, yet fascination. Eventually, to everyone's great relief, Manindi won. It was very exciting.

The people watched as the lizard died. They watched as its blood flowed freely, and heavily stained much of the soil in the area. The ancestor spirits had watched too. They were pleased indeed with Manindi's bravery and ordained that the soil would remain forever red so that people throughout all ages to come would remember the faithful dingo and his amazing victory. This is how it has been.

The people of all groups in that vicinity were of course very relieved and most grateful. Their lives were much more pleasant and peaceful once the giant lizard was dead. On occasion each group planned and performed a corroboree of celebration, which, through mime, retold the story. Before presenting it, they painted and decorated their bodies in red to further show their appreciation. Red, since that time so long ago, has remained a special color for them all.

# The Ningaui

*The Aboriginal people who lived long ago on islands off the north coast of Australia believed that strange little beings called the Ningaui (pronounced Ningoree) shared their islands. The Ningaui, who were said to be about 60 centimetres tall, had long, black hair and unusually big feet. It was believed that the Ningaui hunted and performed rituals similar to those of the north coast Aboriginal people — but they did it all in secret in the darkness of the night.*

The Ningaui kept themselves hidden in the dense jungle growth that bordered the many swamps in the area. It seems that they loved the dark but they did at times light a fire. It is said that if ever an Aboriginal hunter, attracted by one of these fires, accidentally came upon these strange little beings they would all screech and scream terribly. Their voices were said to be high-pitched and shrill. The fire would then magically and mysteriously disappear and the doomed hunter would become forever lost in the darkness and the swamps.

It is said too that the evil little Ningaui would steal any child who strayed too near the swamps. And once a child disappeared she or he would never be seen again. The people living in that area at the time say that they never saw these mysterious little beings but the legends tell us that they often heard them calling, 'Eeh, eeh, eeh,' to each other in the darkness.

The Aboriginal people who lived there in that long ago time wisely avoided the swamp areas, especially after dark.

# Water Peanuts

*Arnhem Land in northern Australia has some very interesting vegetation. Some plants which thrive there do not grow anywhere else. One such plant is called in the Aboriginal language main-goid-bang. The English name for this plant is water peanut. The fruit of this plant has two sections. One tastes like a raw vegetable, such as a potato, while the other section tastes crunchy, like a nut, hence its name. The fruit of the water peanut bush needs to be treated with care and caution. It must be cooked on its own and even kept separate from other food while in storage.*

There are several stories from the Dreaming of the Arnhem Land people which tell about water peanuts. This is one of them.

This story comes from the place known today as Oenpelli. It tells of an Aboriginal man who lived alone in that area long ago when the world was new. He was one of the first people to ever live there. He chose to live there because he dearly loved eating water peanuts and this is where they grew. In fact, he was obsessed with eating water peanuts.

Sometimes, he ate them raw. Sometimes, he cooked them whole. Sometimes, he dried then pounded them into a powder from which he made a damper. He seldom hunted for, or ate, kangaroo or possum meat, other fruits, seeds or berries. He lived almost entirely on water peanuts.

There was a problem, however. In some seasons there was not enough rain to water his precious plants and without a continual supply of water, the water peanut

plants simply do not thrive. The man worried about this for some time. Eventually he realized that if he could cry, cry continually, his tears would water the plants. This seemed the obvious answer, so he began to focus his mind on sad situations to keep the tears falling. One cause for sadness was his loneliness; so he cried about being lonely. He cried until a visitor arrived. The visitor had come to tell him about the death of an old friend. So the man was able to cry for several more days about that.

When his visitor left, he, of course, cried again. When he discovered that his visitor had been bitten by a snake and had died on his journey home, he was able to cry for several more days. Though he was truly sad about all of these happenings, he was pleased to see his precious plants being watered. Eventually, however, he could cry no more. He was lonely, yes, but he had grown used to that. He could no longer find anything sad enough to make him cry.

This concerned him a great deal, for he knew that he had to keep the water peanut plants alive. If he failed they would be lost to future generations forever. Somehow he knew that one day, a long time into the future, a large group of his people would live in that part of Arnhem Land, and they would be wanting water peanuts. So he knew he had to keep the plants alive, no matter what.

After much thought he decided to give up his earthly life for the sake of the water peanut plants. He knew that if he could leave the earth and go to the sky-world he would then be able to raise a little corner of the sky, when needed, to let extra rain fall. The extra

rain would keep the water peanut bushes flourishing. This he managed to do, and do well.

Many generations later, when large numbers of his people, as expected, came to live in Arnhem Land, the ancestor spirit came to them and showed them how to collect and cook and use the water peanuts he had so faithfully nurtured for them. From that time to this, the water peanut man, like thousands of other ancestor spirits, has been there to guide and guard the Oenpelli people, his people, throughout all the days of their lives.

# Why the Black Snake Hides

*One of the many legends which come from the Aboriginal people of Thursday Island tells us how the black snake got its poisonous fangs.*

We have been told that during the Dreaming the black snake had no venom at all in its fangs. It was, it seems, quite harmless. No-one feared the black snake in any way. But the people who lived at this time on Thursday Island did have a great and terrible fear of a giant goanna which shared their world. The goanna was a meat-eater who loved the taste of human flesh. It spent much of its time creeping up on unsuspecting men, women and children. Once it had captured them its great jaws quickly chomped into their helpless bodies. Within minutes, there was no trace left at all. All the people lived in fear and their numbers were dwindling alarmingly.

Several brave hunters went to fight the goanna but none of them was successful. As each came near to make a surprise attack, the giant sniffed their scent. The brave warriors were then unceremoniously eaten, or at the very least severely bitten and left to die from poisonous venom which the goanna unleashed.

## WHY THE BLACK SNAKE HIDES

The wise, old Head Man was very distressed. He wanted very much to rid his island home of this terrible menace, but he was old and sick and no longer strong and quick. There was no way he could fight the goanna and win — or was there? He spent many days considering the problem. After some time a plan came into his head. Bravely, he decided to put it into action.

The Head Man's personal totem was, in fact, the black snake. At this time in history humans were able to interchange bodies with their special totem creature. This he did. As a black snake, he slid off alone towards the cave of the giant goanna. He knew that the goanna was very big and powerful, and in addition very poisonous, but he was not afraid for he did not plan to fight the goanna. He planned to outwit it.

The black snake, as planned, slid clear across the island and hid in a clump of bushes near the goanna's cave. There he waited, still and silent, until the fat, marauding goanna came waddling by. The evil goanna had chomped up several more people that morning. Now, feeling overfull, it had returned to its cave to rest. The little black snake watched as the goanna, as always, sniffed the air. There was no 'human scent' around to worry about, so the giant creature let its ugly body flop heavily onto the floor of the cave. Then it went to sleep.

After a time the goanna began snoring loudly, leaving its great mouth wide open. The black snake, as planned, slithered silently into the cave. Then, quick as a wink, he dived into the goanna's mouth and, with his own small mouth, he dragged out the sac of poisonous venom. He tried of course to spit out the venom but unfortunately it

became firmly lodged in his throat. He then decided that since the venom was there he would bite the goanna several times hoping the poison would work against the creature. This he did.

Then, still in the form of a black snake, the old man hid outside the cave. He was prepared to stay for several weeks to see what effect, if any, the poison would have. He saw in time that the goanna did not die but he did most definitely change, quite miraculously, and completely for the better!

The poison had worked in a strange way on the giant creature. Unbelievably, from that time on, the goanna no longer wished to eat meat or be vicious. The black snake watched for days as the goanna began to shuffle about peacefully and slowly, quite content, from then on, to eat grasses, fruits and small insects. This was a marvellous result.

But what of the brave old Head Man? He was, of course, very pleased. By taking away the poison he had been able to take away the awful power of the goanna. Although he knew that his people would now be safe, he realized sadly that he would never be able to return to them or their camp site ever again. He could not return because he now had in his mouth the deadly poisonous venom. He would therefore be a danger to his people.

The old man continued to live on as a black snake. He watched from afar the progress of his people but, because he did not wish to accidentally harm anyone with his poison, he continued to hide as much as possible from them all.

Many black snakes live on Thursday Island today. They are still quite poisonous, but they are feared very little for they try, like the old man, to hide as much as possible from the people there.

# The Kangaroo Who Danced

*There are legends from the early days of the
Dreaming which tell us that the kangaroos once
walked on all four legs as other animals do. One
story about these early creatures and this period of
time comes from the Kamilaroi people of northern
New South Wales.*

As you can imagine most kangaroos kept well away from all the Aboriginal camp sites at all times. They knew only too well that the hunters were quick and skilfull with their spears. This legend tells of one particular kangaroo who was not as timid as the others. Under cover of darkness he often crept stealthily to the edge of the people's living area. There he would stand, well out of sight, and watch as the Kamilaroi danced an exciting, sacred corroboree. He was fascinated by their music.

One particular evening the kangaroo witnessed a very special corroboree of celebration. Fires had been lit in a circle. These cast a mysterious glow on all, as men with their bodies painted in stripes of red, yellow, and white, began to dance, dive, and chant dramatically. The kangaroo felt a strange excitement. He watched and listened to the throb of the percussion instruments, the accompanying chant of the women, and the steady clap, clapping of hands and thighs. As the action continued the

dancers seemed to become as one with the leaping flames. Their movements became even wilder and their chanting more fervent as the rhythmic throb of the bull-roarer began.

The sights, the sounds, and the aura of magic and purpose which abounded, seemed to intoxicate the kangaroo. His mind began to whirl. His heart began to beat faster. Suddenly he found his four feet were tapping the wild rhythm and he felt gripped by a strange fever, an uncontrollable urge to join the dancers.

'No, no,' he said to himself, 'Calm yourself.' But he did not listen; without further hesitation he dashed from his hiding place into the firelight, into the centre of the corroboree. As he did so, he subconsciously straightened up like the men, standing and dancing on two legs while using his tail as a balance.

As you can imagine the people were quite amazed, but they were all so involved in the drama, the music and the rhythm themselves that they accepted this strange occurrence as a mystical illusion, a magical phenomenon of some kind. Meanwhile the kangaroo became totally caught up in the dance and the atmosphere and he leapt and kicked and dived just as the men did. The people watching clapped and chanted more fiercely as the corroboree proceeded. At times the men joined hands with the dancing kangaroo and drew him into the inner circle.

The corroboree, in all its glory, continued on through many, many hours of darkness. The wide-eyed children, against their will, eventually fell asleep. At last, near to dawn, the dancers and the watchers began to show signs

of exhaustion. When the bull-roarer finally ceased its wail everyone collapsed to the ground, glad to rest.

It was then, to their further amazement, that everyone realized that the kangaroo was not something their wild imaginings had created. They saw that he was very real indeed and that he too was exhausted from his astounding and amazing dance. They all watched in silence as the kangaroo lay motionless on the ground beside the men. He was totally out of breath.

For a short time the scene was peaceful but, before the weary kangaroo could regain his strength and escape to the safety of the bush, one of the Elders rushed at him and threw a large net over his head. The kangaroo began to tremble with fear; he knew what was about to happen.

'This kangaroo will have to die,' the Elder announced angrily. 'He has stood on his hind legs like a human; he has invaded our privacy and shared our sacred, secret experience. He cannot be allowed to live. He must die before dawn.'

The other group members listened in horror as the death sentence was pronounced. Though they knew that this was what the law demanded, it seemed so unfair and so unkind.

'No! No! No!' the people all whispered; but not one of them dared to stand and argue with this particular Elder. All were stunned and still and terribly sad because the grey light of dawn had already begun to appear. The kangaroo of course began to deeply regret his lack of caution. Even so, he felt it had been a wonderful,

incredible experience. He decided that he could not, would not change it, even if he were able.

As the kangaroo resigned himself sadly to his fate, the eerie silence was broken by another Elder who stood and began to speak. This Elder explained that he had been considering the whole situation carefully. He then stated most strongly that he felt the kangaroo should be rewarded not punished.

'Why should this be so?' demanded the Elder who had first spoken.

'Because the kangaroo has come to us in friendship,' answered the second Elder. 'I feel that the ancestor spirits above would have rejoiced to see such a celebration of life and unity,' he added.

'That's right. That's right,' shouted all the people. 'Let him live! Let the kangaroo live!' The kangaroo lay silently among them, still trapped by the giant net.

'Let us call on the ancestor spirits,' suggested the Elder. 'Let them decide what should be done.'

Suddenly the bull-roarer began to wail though no one twirled it and a spirit voice boomed from the sky, 'The kangaroo must be allowed to live and henceforth he and all his kind will continue to travel in an upright position, on their hind legs. Let this be a reminder to all, throughout time, that your creator expects you to respect all living creatures. Kill what you need for food, but otherwise cause no harm.'

The message of the mysterious echoing voice from the sky was received with great relief and joy. The net was loosed immediately and the kangaroo struggled quickly to his feet. As expected, he found he now stood

naturally and solidly on his two hind legs. It was a good feeling. The people stood and cheered as the kangaroo hopped proudly away from them, free and unharmed, but completely changed.

News of the amazing event spread from this group to others and forever after each person thought about the famous corroboree whenever they saw a kangaroo hopping about, as they still do today, on two legs not four.

The people of that particular group later created their own special kangaroo dance. This they danced on special occasions as a reminder of that amazing night. Many other Aboriginal groups down through the ages have added segments of this special kangaroo dance to their own corroborees.

# Glossary

**ancestor spirit**  guardian angel of Aboriginal people; has magical powers.

**awl**  tool for making small holes in timber or leather. Made of bone, stone or shell by Traditional Aborigines.

**brolga**  light grey bird of the crane species, known for its rhythmic dancing movements (Aboriginal name).

**bull-roarer**  a long thin strip of wood with a cord at one end, by which it is whirled rapidly to create an exotic wailing sound. Used by Aboriginal men during sacred Traditional ceremonies.

**Byamee**  the name given to the wise and helpful god and creator of several Aboriginal areas in Central New South Wales. Well known from legends telling of constant involvement with earth's people.

**camp site**  the area surrounding the cooking fires. Each Aboriginal camp site was occupied temporarily but re-used constantly.

**clan**  a subdivision or section within a large Aboriginal group. The Wiradjuri group, for example, had many clans.

**coolamon**  an Aboriginal container carved from timber.

**corroboree**  a rhythmic, ceremonial dance, including mime, stomping, chanting — performed by several Aboriginal people in unison — usually well choreographed and practised.

**damper**  an unleavened loaf or scone, typically cooked on an open fire.

**didgeridoo**  a highly decorated instrument made from a long hollowed out sapling. Unique to Australian Aborigines. Used in the Traditional period in Northern Australia only.

**dilly bags**  bags woven from strips of sinew, leather, stringy-bark or vines. Used as carry bags by all Traditional Aboriginal people, mostly the women.

**dingo**  wild, native dog. Trained, in the Traditional period, to assist Aboriginal hunters.

**dreeing**  the wailing, rhythmic sound produced by the didgeridoos.

| | |
|---|---|
| **earth oven** | used by Traditional Aboriginal people to cook large amounts of meat — consists of hot coals in a pit with a fire burning around and above. |
| **echidna** | a small egg-laying, ant-eating Australian mammal with a covering of spines (spikes) — has a long slender snout, no teeth. |
| **Elders** | the most respected, older men of an Aboriginal group. They formed a council, governed/advised members of group and exercised total power. |
| **emu** | a large Australian bird resembling an ostrich — can't fly but can run fast. |
| **eucalyptus** | indigenous Australian tree. |
| **firestick** | A small smoldering slow burning hardwood log — relit and carried from camp site to camp site. Used to light new fires. |
| **goanna** | a large Australian monitor lizard, grows to 2 metres in Eastern states. |
| **grind** | the crushing action used by Aboriginal women to create flour from grass seeds. Also a method used by Aboriginal men to sharpen awls, spearheads etc, by rubbing the tool on something rough or abrasive, usually sandstone. |
| **Head Man** | most significant member of Council of Elders in Aboriginal group. Makes the final decisions, all-powerful but usually wise and just. |
| **inner circle** | used in the context of this book to mean the most sacred section. |
| **kangaroo** | Australian mammal, many species; has small fore legs, very strong hind legs which give leaping power, uses tail for balance. Female kangaroo has a pouch in which she raises her young (Aboriginal name). |
| **kelp** | brown-coloured seaweed; many species, some grow as long as 5 metres. |
| **kinship-linked** | share the same totem. |
| **koala** | a furry grey Australian mammal, lives in trees, eats eucalyptus leaves, nurtures its young in a pouch (Aboriginal name). |

| | |
|---|---|
| **kookaburra** | an Australian meat-eating bird of the kingfisher species, has unique 'laughing-like' call (Aboriginal name). |
| **kylies** | see tap-sticks. |
| **ocher** | a mixture of iron, lime and clay in yellow, brown and red tones. Used in body, bark and rock painting by Aboriginal people of the Traditional period. |
| **pipi** | Australian shellfish (Aboriginal name). |
| **possum** | any of various Australian phalangers, small and furry, hunt at night, carry their young in a pouch. |
| **ritual** | a form or system of spiritual rites. |
| **rock python** | special species of python, likes to hide, kills by crushing. |
| **sky-world** | regarded by Traditional Aboriginal people as a living area in another dimension. Sometimes called the spirit world. |
| **spinifex grass** | sharp, single-bladed grass, grows in desert areas. |
| **stringy-bark** | a species of eucalypt (gum) tree; has bark which hangs off in strips. |
| **tap-sticks** | percussion instruments, used by all Aboriginal people to enforce the needed rhythm when chanting and/or dancing; usually decorated lavishly. Known also as kylies. |
| **totem** | the sacred symbol of an Aboriginal person or group, could be animal, bird, mineral or plant associated. Spirit-given. |
| **waddy** | Aboriginal club, used in combat, to stun animals, or to crush rocks. |
| **wallaby** | Australian animal, similar in appearance to kangaroo, though smaller. Female carries her young in a pouch (Aboriginal name). |
| **Wandjina** | the god and creator of the Aboriginal areas along the Western Australian coast. Well known through legends. |
| **willy wagtail** | small Australian bird, inquisitive, quick, has characteristic tail movement. |
| **wombat** | Australian burrowing mammal, small, thick, heavy body, short legs. Female carries young in her pouch (Aboriginal name). |

# Also by JEAN A ELLIS

For the Aboriginal people of Australia the Dreamtime is the beginning of the world but it is also yesterday, today and forever. From the Dreamtime comes a rich and wonderful lore that tells of the creation of earth, sun, moon and stars, why the animals look the way they do, how the Great Ancestor Spirits loved and looked after their people. This collection of legends from different areas of Australia reflects the vivid imagination, strong sense of drama and above all the intimate understanding of nature that is characteristic of the Aboriginal people of Australia.

*From the Dreamtime* is Jean Ellis' first collection of Aboriginal legends and a companion to her new collection, *This Is The Dreaming*.

CollinsDove
An imprint of HarperCollins*Publishers*

ISBN 1 86371 016 7

# Also by JEAN A ELLIS

AUSTRALIA'S
ABORIGINAL
HERITAGE

JEAN A.ELLIS

The continent of Australia is a unique ancient landscape that has been home for the Aboriginal people for over 40,000 years. With their adherance to the spiritual rituals of their Dreaming, the guiding presence of their ancestors, and their mystical ties with the natural world, the Aboriginal people have given Australia a powerful and enduring heritage.

In *Australia's Aboriginal Heritage*, Jean A Ellis, author of *From the Dreamtime* and *This Is the Dreaming*, presents a beautifully illustrated account of Aboriginal lifestyle and culture, both traditional and transitional. Embracing art, history, spirituality, and even contemporary Aboriginal poetry, this is a book to treasure.

CollinsDove
An imprint of HarperCollins*Publishers*

ISBN 1 86371 262 3